Discovering Links

Ron Benson

Lynn Bryan

Kim Newlove

Charolette Player

Liz Stenson

CONSULTANTS

Susan Elliott

Diane Lomond

Ken MacInnis

Elizabeth Parchment

PRENTICE HALL GINN CANADA

Contents

Bibliography

 Selections with this symbol are available on audio.

 This symbol indicates student writing.

 Canadian selections are marked with this symbol.

Aboriginal Heritage Links

by Karolyn Smardz

Digging Up the Past

There are many ways of reaching out to touch the past, and many ways of discovering our links to people who lived before us. Archaeologists study objects, called *artifacts,* and other clues left behind by peoples who lived in earlier times. They do this in order to learn more about what life was like a hundred or a thousand or ten thousand years ago.

Archaeologists use many different scientific methods to gather their evidence. However, when most people hear the word "archaeology" they think about archaeological excavations, or *digs*. In a dig, archaeologists seek to answer a question or series of questions about how people lived in a specific place at a certain time in the past. First they lay out a grid of squares so they can measure, map, and record the exact location of every single artifact and clue that they find on the site. Then they carefully remove layer after layer of soil, recording each find as they go, and sifting every bucketful of dirt to see if any tiny object was missed during the digging. After that, the artifacts are analyzed. Their relationship to each other and to other features of the site, such as hearths or the remains of buildings, help the archaeologist understand more about how people used the area in earlier times. Archaeologists use many different methods to analyze artifacts. One of the most useful is Carbon-14 dating, which measures how much of the element Carbon-14 is left in artifacts made of organic substances such as bone. Scientists also can judge the ages of tools such as spear points by looking at similar tools found at other sites.

An archaeological dig, then, isn't just a treasure hunt for "stuff" earlier people left behind in the ground. It is a slow, careful search for clues about how people behaved, interacted with their environment, and survived at a particular time in the past.

Introduction

Canada has been occupied by human beings for many thousands of years. Evidence for the activities of Aboriginal Peoples has been found in every part of the country. Here, three special Canadian sites are used to show how archaeology develops links with people who lived in the past. All are sites where Aboriginal Canadians have worked with archaeologists to discover more about, and teach others about, what life was like for their own peoples in earlier times.

Head-Smashed-In Buffalo Jump

Head-Smashed-In Buffalo Jump is the oldest and best-preserved buffalo kill site in the world. This world-famous archaeological site is located about eighteen kilometres west of Fort MacLeod, Alberta. Here, Aboriginal Peoples—beginning 5700 years ago and continuing into the early 1800s—used to drive herds of buffalo off the top of a ten-metre-high cliff to kill them. The hunters did this to get food and other resources they needed, such as hides and bone from the buffalo.

At Head-Smashed-In, archaeologists concentrated on excavating camp sites where buffalo meat, hides, bones, horns, and hoofs were processed in order to learn more about how the Plains Peoples preserved the meat for food, and made tools, clothing, and other items from the buffalo. Thousands of artifacts were found at the site. These included bone tools, stone arrow or spear points, horn containers, and ceremonial objects such as painted skulls and hoof rattles. Stone tools dated to nine thousand years ago have also been found.

▲ Excavation work at Head-Smashed-In Buffalo Jump. The Interpretive Centre is in the background.

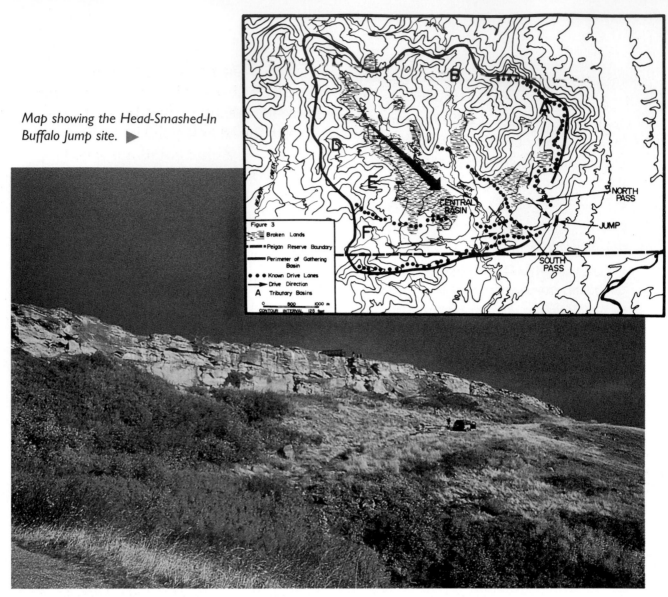

Map showing the Head-Smashed-In Buffalo Jump site. ▶

Figure 3
- ≡ Broken Lands
- ■ Peigan Reserve Boundary
- — Perimeter of Gathering Basin
- ● ● ● Known Drive Lanes
- → Drive Direction
- A Tributary Basins

CREEK · BEAVER CREEK · NORTH PASS · JUMP · SOUTH PASS · CENTRAL BASIN

0   500   1000 m
CONTOUR INTERVAL 125 feet

▲ *The cliff at Head-Smashed-In.*

A wealth of information about the culture and lifestyle of the Plains Aboriginal Peoples of Canada has been revealed at Head-Smashed-In Buffalo Jump. This information is now presented in a wonderful Interpretive Centre by Blackfoot interpreters, descendants of the Plains Peoples who once hunted there. Visitors can view the artifacts found and learn about the different types of scientific analysis used in the work, such as Carbon-14 dating.

One of the most important pieces of information revealed at the site is the close and positive relationship the Plains Aboriginal Peoples had with their environment. Although many buffalo were killed each time a herd was driven over the cliff, almost no part of the animals' bodies was wasted. These earlier Aboriginal Peoples can teach us much about sustainable living in our environment.

▲ Students sit around <u>X</u>á:ytem, an important spiritual and cultural landmark to the Stó:lō people.

<u>X</u>á:ytem: A Stó:lō Peoples' Site

<u>X</u>á:ytem (HAY-tum), a site overlooking the Fraser River near Mission, British Columbia, is a wonderful example of an archaeological site that was saved through co-operation. Here, scientists from the University of British Columbia and members of the Stó:lō Coast Salish First Nations worked together with a responsible developer, who stopped the bulldozers at his subdivision to salvage <u>X</u>á:ytem, also known as the Hatzic Rock.

According to Salish oral history, <u>X</u>á:ytem is the place where four chiefs were turned to stone by important spirits called the <u>X</u>a:ls (HAALS). Tradition says that the four chiefs still reside within the rock, so it is an extremely sacred site for the Stó:lō, the modern Aboriginal Peoples of the area.

Another important find at the site was an ancient house walled with gravel, and built part way into the ground for insulation. The house contained several hearths, and stone arrow or spear points and stone tools were found. Tools made from obsidian, a type of volcanic glass found in Oregon, were also found, evidence that the people who built their home at Hatzic more than five thousand years ago were part of a well-developed culture with extensive trading networks.

At <u>X</u>á:ytem, the Stó:lō Coast Salish First Nations have chosen to honor and explore the heritage left behind by their ancestors. They have developed an educational program to help visitors understand what has been discovered about <u>X</u>á:ytem and

▲ Excavating the remains of a large house dating between five and six thousand years old.

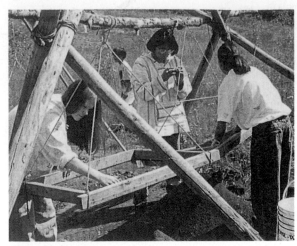

▲ *Students taking part at an archaeology workshop at the X̱á:ytem Interpretive Centre.*

the nearby house site. It is a place where spirits and science reside together to help us develop links to our heritage as Canadians.

The Angik Archaeological Field Project

In the Western Arctic, archaeologists and the Community Education Council of Paulatuk have come together to excavate the Angik Archaeological Site on the Paulatuk Peninsula, near Yellowknife, Northwest Territories.

Parks Canada and the Prince of Wales Northern Heritage Centre are working with local Inuit students to discover and conserve their rich heritage. The site they have chosen to excavate contains two sod huts built within the last hundred years. Learning about these will help researchers understand more about

Inuit life on the Paulatuk Peninsula in the early twentieth century. The people who lived in the sod houses at Angik were the cultural heirs to thousands of years of Inuit occupation at the mouth of the Mackenzie River.

This tradition is being studied nearby at Kittigazuit, a much older site than Angik. It was home to thousands of people over the centuries. Like Head-Smashed-In Buffalo Jump, Kittigazuit was a hunting site. Here, however, the animal hunted was the beluga whale. There are still Inuit who remember their families moving to the area once a year to hunt the

Lee Ruben with disc of bowhead whale vertebra. ▶

beluga, so archaeologists can compare evidence from the dig with Inuit oral history to gain greater understanding of a unique way of life.

The excavation at Kittigazuit has brought to light thousands of artifacts

◄ *Part of an internal structure of a house.*

made from parts of whales, as well as tools used to process the whale meat, fat, and other products. The Inuit used every bit of the whale that they could to help themselves live and prosper in such a cold climate.

The artifacts from the Angik Project Site, however, reflect a mix of Inuit and European-influenced tools and customs. They include parts of a cast-iron stove, mass-produced buttons, and iron nails, along with a traditional bone fishing lure and other objects carved from caribou bone.

The Angik Archaeology Field Project represents an important blend of science and oral history. Students and archaeologists are seeking to form a link with the thousands of years of past Inuit culture on the Paulatuk Peninsula.

Conclusion

Archaeology offers all of us a way to discover links to the past, and to examine artifacts and other evidence buried hundreds or even thousands of years ago. It also helps illustrate information contained in oral traditions. Because of the co-operation between First Nations Peoples and archaeologists at these three sites, all Canadians have a remarkable opportunity to learn more about our nation's Aboriginal heritage.

◄ *Lee Ruben's journal entry, written the day he found the whale vertebra.*

Angik Archaeology Field Project

✓ You had an exciting day!

STUDENT DAILY JOURNAL   August 1996

Site: NiRm-1 (Site)   **DAY #3**

Name: LEE Ruben   Date: Aug-14-96

Weather conditions: North East am. pm south west wind
sunny. A little bit of cloud's

Today's activities: Today I found A whale bone.
and a big, 2x4 wood

What I learned today: I learnd Everything

What was good about today: found A whale Disk

cts recovered today: Whale Back bone called whale Disk
and a 2x4 wood,

g (draw an artifact you recovered today or a scene of something you learned at the excavation today)

(A DISK)

(2x4 wood)

Inset

ld like to suggest for tomorrow: A Level to see how wide
the site

Five Hundred Years Later: Newfoundland Celebrates Cabot's Voyage

by Liz Stenson

Hundreds of years ago, on the island we now call Newfoundland, lived the tall, black-eyed, black-haired Beothuk people. They adorned themselves and their belongings with a mixture of red ochre and oil to ward off the cold in winter and as protection from insects in summer. Because of this, they are often referred to as the Red Paint People. The

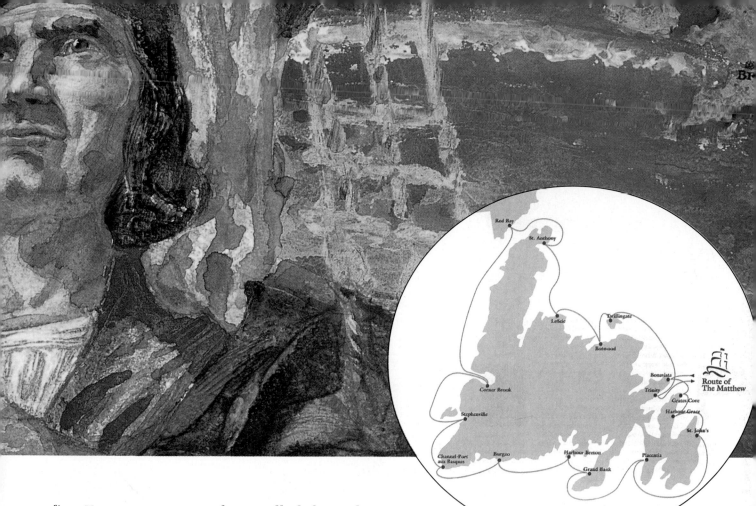

first Europeans to see them called them the "Red Indians." Now extinct, the Beothuks were skilled hunters and fishers who had learned to live well with the land and the sea.

Imagine the surprise and consternation of these people when, one June day in 1497, they spied a great three-masted boat on the horizon, its square and triangular sails billowing in the wind. It was unlike any boat they had ever seen. Perhaps they retreated into the forest, for when the captain of the ship came ashore, he found only a path leading into the woods, a spot where a fire had been made, some animal snares, and a red-painted stick that might have been a netting needle. Anxious about these signs of life, he and his crew stayed only long enough to take on fresh water and to erect a cross and banners bearing the arms of the King of England and of the Pope. Thus Cabot claimed this land for England.

The *Matthew* Visit

The *Matthew* spent forty-six days visiting seventeen ports around the coasts of Newfoundland and Labrador. Everywhere she went, the occasion was marked with special events.

The final port of call was the village of Trinity, which is the location of the earliest permanent settlement based entirely on the fishery. The people of Trinity planned to celebrate with a banquet, a concert, and a special exhibition on early sailing ships.

Statue of Cabot

This statue stands on the headland at Bonavista overlooking Cabot's "new founde lande."

The Codfish

It was the cod that first brought Europeans to Canada's shores, leading eventually to the first successful colonies. The cod was valued for its fine taste, firm white flesh, and good storage qualities. The early cod fishermen went out in small row boats. A large weighted, but often baitless, hook would be let over the side and jigged up and down until taken by the fish. The fish were then either packed in barrels of salt and water or salted then dried in the sun. Sun-dried cod became Canada's first export to the world. For almost five centuries, the economies of Newfoundland and other Atlantic communities centred on the cod fishery.

Who was this sea captain who landed on these shores, the first European to do so since the Viking explorers over five hundred years previously? And why had he come?

Giovanni Caboto, or John Cabot, as he was called in English, was an Italian navigator and explorer. He was born, likely in Genoa, around 1450. His family moved to Venice when he was a boy. He grew up to be a merchant, trading goods between Venice and the Arab countries, and gained a reputation as a skilled and experienced mariner. Around 1495, Cabot moved to England. People at that time were continually searching for new ways to sail to the Orient, where they could trade for spices, jewels, and silks. Cabot, perhaps inspired by tales of Christopher Columbus's voyage, wanted to discover a western route to the Orient by sailing across the Atlantic.

In 1496, Cabot was authorized by Henry VII, King of England, to lead a venture to find unknown lands to the west. The merchants of Bristol, a port in England, put up the money to finance the trip, for they, too, were eager about the prospect of trade in the Orient. On or around May 2, 1497, Cabot and a small crew set sail from Bristol in the *Matthew*. Some historians say his three sons were also aboard.

The *Matthew* was a *caravel*, a small and seaworthy ship with a high bow and stern and a mixture of square and *lateen* (triangular) sails. The voyage across the North Atlantic is believed to have taken thirty-five days. Life on board would have been very hard. While there was enough food to last seven or eight months, it likely consisted of salted meat and fish, dried biscuits, dried beans and peas, and beer. What a boring diet that must have made! The *Matthew* had no cabins for the crew. They slept anywhere they could find, perhaps curling up in a corner of the deck. Fortunately, the crossing was relatively easy, with only one reported gale. On June 24, Cabot landed on the North American coast. While historians do not agree on the actual landing site, most believe it to have been Cape Bonavista, Newfoundland.

For the next month, Cabot and his crew explored the Newfoundland coast, finding the area we now know as The Grand Banks, a shallow shelf in the ocean that is a favorite breeding ground for cod. The waters were teeming with fish, so plentiful that the crew caught them by merely lowering weighted baskets over the sides of the ship and pulling them up full of fish.

In August, Cabot returned to Bristol with news of the amazing bounty of fish in the new land. The king and the Bristol investors were delighted. The king rewarded Cabot with the sum of ten pounds, a lot of money in those days, and a yearly pension for "hym that founde the new isle." He also authorized a second expedition of five ships and many more men. Early in 1498, Cabot set sail once again. This time he did not return, and while we don't know for sure what happened, it is believed that he perished somewhere off the coast of Newfoundland.

Cabot's news of this "new founde lande" and its abundant fishing grounds soon became known in Europe. In the years that followed, fleets of fishing boats set sail every spring to reap the abundant fish harvest, particularly cod. It was preserved in barrels of salt and water, or salted and sun-dried. The sailors found not only cod, but whales diving in the coastal waters, seals and walruses perched on the rocky shores, and salmon in the inland rivers. They called this new place Newfoundland. When Sir Humphrey Gilbert, an English explorer, arrived in the summer

City of St. John's

Cabot landed in Newfoundland on June 24, which is the day of the Christian religious holiday St. John the Baptist Day. Today, St. John's, Newfoundland's capital city, bears that name.

Cabot Tower

The Cabot Tower, constructed for the 400th anniversary of Cabot's voyage, is a treasured National Historic Site.

The New *Matthew*

Building a wooden ship takes a great deal of work. Even with modern power tools and heavy lifting equipment, it took a dozen skilled shipwrights two years to complete the new *Matthew*. The ship was built right in Bristol harbor, a short distance from where the original ship would have been built five centuries earlier. Then, the medieval craftsman had a difficult time, relying only on hand tools. One of the most common tools was the adze, used to shape and trim timbers. The adze is a versatile and effective tool and the builders of the new *Matthew* still used them. The keel of the *Matthew* was laid in the summer of 1993 and the boat completed in March 1996. It cost approximately one million pounds (two and a quarter million Canadian dollars) to build the *Matthew*.

colony at St. John's in 1583, he found there "men of all nations," though mainly from England, France, Spain, and Portugal. Today, many Newfoundlanders are descendants of these early fishermen.

The year 1997 marked the 500th anniversary of Cabot's landing in Newfoundland. Many events were planned to commemorate and celebrate this historic occasion and to focus on Newfoundland's cultural identity and sea-going heritage. There were song-and-dance festivals featuring international performers, art shows, historical discussions and pageants, seafood suppers, street dances, and regattas and other sports events. If there was a way to celebrate, the Newfoundlanders thought of it!

Perhaps the most notable of these events was the arrival of an exact replica of the *Matthew*. The ship was built in Bristol, England, using many of the same shipbuilding techniques as would have been used when the original *Matthew* was built. On May 2, the same day Cabot sailed, and with thousands of people looking on, she left Bristol harbor. She set course to follow Cabot's reputed route to Newfoundland. On June 24 she arrived in Bonavista, led into the harbor by a flotilla of hundreds of ships from Newfoundland, Labrador, Canada, the United States, and beyond. Queen Elizabeth and thousands of Newfoundlanders were there to greet them. What a wonderful grand celebration it was!

The Queen greets members of the new Matthew's *crew.* ▶

On the Way to Canada

by Margaret J. Anderson
Illustrated by Peter Ferguson

Elspeth MacDonald's parents planned to leave Scotland to start a new life in Canada, where they had relatives. Before the family could leave Glasgow, both parents died. Elspeth knew that the authorities would separate her and her brother, Robbie, so she decided to run away. She had the steamship tickets and a little money, and she knew that her uncle lived in a place called Manitoba.

The children travelled by train to Liverpool, and joined the throng of people waiting to board the ship bound for Canada. To keep Robbie quiet, Elspeth invented a hide-and-seek game about Shadow Bairns who had to hide so they wouldn't catch them.

They slept that night on the train, which had been shunted into a siding near Liverpool Station because there was nowhere else for the passengers to go. Every hotel and boarding house within kilometres was full.

The following morning, the two children joined the vast crowds hurrying from all parts of the city toward the dock where the *Lake Manitoba* waited. There was no need to ask the way. Elspeth could hardly believe that so many people could all be going to Canada.

About the time the children joined the throng pushing toward the gangplanks, the Reverend Isaac Moses Barr was looking down from the vantage point of the deck of the *Lake Manitoba*. Seeing the crowds below, he felt like Moses of old, leading his people to the Promised Land. He didn't look like Moses, for he was stocky, and clean shaven except for a small mustache that drooped over the corners of his mouth. He peered nearsightedly through round spectacles that were misting over in the light rain. Around his neck was a clerical collar, and on his head a white cap.

Isaac Barr wasn't worrying about how to squeeze more than two thousand people into a boat equipped for less than eight hundred, nor how to feed them in dining rooms that wouldn't accommodate a quarter their number. He scarcely noticed the mountains of luggage still piling up on the dock. Instead he was congratulating himself that he was giving so many people a chance to escape the smoky industrial cities of England. He was strengthening the ties between Britain and Canada. He smiled complacently at the thought that he was changing the course of history.

These exalted thoughts were interrupted by a nervous young man in the uniform of a head steward. "Mr. Barr, sir! There's too many people wanting to come on board, sir. There's more than we have beds and bedding for."

"Then they will have to share bunks or sleep on the floor."

"Some of the stewards have deserted the ship, sir. They're afraid, sir. There's too many people."

"Then hire more stewards from among the passengers," Mr. Barr answered impatiently. "That will solve both problems—more stewards and fewer passengers."

The young man was bewildered. Surely Mr. Barr must be joking, but there was no hint of a smile on Barr's broad face as he looked down at the waiting crowd.

"They're still coming," said the steward.

"Aye, they're still coming," echoed Barr. "And there is a great land waiting for them—a great fertile land under the dome of God's own sky. Have you seen the cities these people come from—their horizons limited by the walls of factories and tenement buildings, the sky stained black with smoke belching from a hundred chimneys?"

Mr. Barr's voice rose and fell as if he were talking from a pulpit. The steward shuffled nervously, waiting for a chance to interrupt.

"This immigration scheme will be a pattern for other people to follow," Mr. Barr went on. "We're changing lives. You're seeing history being made."

"But what about all these people, sir?"

"Let them come on board."

The gangplanks were lowered and people pushed forward, each one determined to have a place on the ship. There had been rumors circulating all morning that Barr had sold more passages than the boat could hold. One look at the waiting crowds seemed to confirm this.

Elspeth could feel the surge of movement when the first passengers were allowed on the ship somewhere far ahead. She was surrounded by tall men in heavy coats, smelling of wet wool and tobacco. The suitcase was hard to manage, and she worried about getting separated from Robbie. He was having his own troubles, being continually shoved aside and buffeted by suitcases and hampers.

As they were pushed nearer the ship, Elspeth tried to plan what she would say to the ticket collector. It should be easy to convince him that she and Rob had been separated from their parents in this crush, but how was she to find out where they should go on the boat? Was she supposed to have tickets for rooms or beds? She looked up at the side of the ship, rising above the dock like a great white wall. Was it like a train inside, with lots of seats?

Her worries were interrupted by a small but urgent request from Robbie.

"Robbie, you've got to wait!" said Elspeth, desperately looking at the mob of people hemming them in.

"I can't wait," said Robbie tearfully.

"It won't be long now," Elspeth lied, knowing that it could well be hours before they were on the boat.

"I can't wait!" said Robbie again, and promptly wet his blue serge trousers.

Right then, Elspeth decided that running away had been a mistake. There were more problems than she could cope with. When she got on the boat she'd tell the ticket collector that they were by themselves. Let *him* worry about Rob's wet trousers. With that decision made, it was easier to wait her turn to board the *Lake Manitoba*.

They were squashed tighter now, so tight that Elspeth could not even look down at her own feet, but she eventually felt the edge of the gangplank and shuffled forward and up. The travelling bag caught on a ridge of board nailed crosswise on the ramp. She felt the pressure of the crowd behind her as she struggled to free it. The handle was slipping from her grasp, but she managed to jerk the bag up. "Hang on to me, Robbie!" she shouted, but her words were lost, muffled by the crush of bodies around her.

At last they were on the deck. Elspeth looked wildly around for Robbie, only to find that he was right beside her, flushed and tousled, but much less worried and frightened than she was. There was no sign of any official looking at tickets, so Elspeth and Robbie joined the crowd pouring down the stairway. When they saw some other children, they instinctively followed them, and found that all families with children were lodged together in the middle hold.

Elspeth felt vaguely disappointed that the boat wasn't more like the train. There the seats had been covered in soft red velvet and the little lamp fixtures had been gold. Here everything was of raw wood and bare boards, as if it were still being built. The hold was partitioned off by upright posts. Boards nailed to these formed crude bunks, sometimes two deep, sometimes three. Instead of mattresses there was loose straw, and the floor was covered with sawdust.

The hold was a huge room, dimly lit by paraffin lamps. As more and more people crowded in, it seemed smaller and became unbearably hot and noisy. People were claiming bunks, spreading their belongings around, shouting at their children. Tentatively, Elspeth set their bundles on a bottom bunk, but a woman immediately told her to move along because that bunk was taken.

In the far corner, Elspeth spotted a narrow opening between the bunks on the end wall and those on the side. Wriggling into it, she found that the ends of the two sets of bunks and the side of the ship formed a space like a tiny room. Pulling Robbie in beside her, she whispered, "This is where the Shadow Bairns are going to live."

Robbie liked their corner. Right away he began to build Pig-Bear, his favorite toy, a castle out of the sawdust on the floor. Elspeth filched some straw from neighboring bunks, just in case they had to sleep there on the floor. She hoped that once everyone was settled she would be able to claim a leftover bunk without causing any fuss, but the way people were still pouring in there weren't going to be any bunks left. Already arguments and even fights were breaking out. People were being forced to give up some of the bunks they had claimed and put two or three children in one bed.

Elspeth spread their blankets and sorted out their clothes. She helped Robbie change his trousers, laying aside the wet ones until she could find out where to wash them. Getting on the boat now seemed so easy that she was ready to cope again. She wouldn't tell anyone they were alone—not yet. After all, she had even thought of bringing along a bar of yellow laundry soap.

The bunks on either side were occupied now, but no one paid any attention to them. One woman hung blankets over the end of her bunks, which made their corner very dark.

"Pig-Bear can't see," Robbie complained. "And I'm too hot. I want a drink of water."

"I'll get you a drink soon," Elspeth promised, wondering what they were going to do about meals. She was beginning to realize there was a lot she didn't know. "We'll go back up and take a look around, but you're to stay right beside me."

"Like a Shadow Bairn," Robbie said, nodding solemnly.

They crawled out of their corner and made their way through the crowded hold. The first flight of stairs was more like a ladder than a staircase. They had to push their way between people who were still on their way down. Two more flights brought them to the deck.

It was a relief to be outside. A thin drizzle of rain was falling, but the day seemed bright in contrast to the gloom below. They stood in a sheltered place between a lifeboat and the rail, absorbed in the bustling activity all around them. Passengers still hurried up the gangplanks, cranes swung precarious loads of luggage from the dock to the hold, and a mob of gulls was fighting over a basket of bread that had burst open on the dock. The smell of the sea, the wet salt wind, and the cries of the birds reminded Elspeth of their faraway home in the Highlands. For a moment, even she who had so little to leave behind suffered a pang of homesickness, but that was forgotten when a straggling band assembled on the dock played "God be with you till we meet again."

"They're singing to us!" Robbie said, jumping up and down with excitement and clapping his hands.

The pulse of the engines and the shudder of the boat drowned out the last quavering notes. A cheer went up from those staying on the shore, answered by a louder cheer from the deck. When the ship pulled away and the people on the dock were just a dark blur, all waving white handkerchiefs, Robbie was still waving back. He thought that everyone was saying goodbye to him.

Elspeth watched the receding shore. *They* couldn't get Robbie now. She put her arm protectively around his shoulders, pulling him closer to her. If only Mama and Papa could be here too. She tried to shake off the black feeling of loneliness that slipped over her when she thought of her parents. She turned to Robbie. "We've done it, Robbie! We ran away and no one stopped us!" But somewhere in her mind came the answering thought—no one really cared. Abruptly, Elspeth turned her back on England and pulled Robbie over to the stairs.

At the bottom of the first flight they passed a dining room where a steward was setting out a tub of ship biscuits and another of hard-boiled eggs. As soon as his back was turned, Elspeth dashed forward and shoved four eggs into her pockets. She took a biscuit for each of them.

"Was it all right to take them?" Robbie asked nervously when Elspeth divided the spoils back in the hold. "Won't they be angry?"

"It's our supper. It's meant for us," Elspeth reassured him. "It's just better to eat it here by ourselves. I'll take our mugs and fetch tea, but you wait here."

The ship biscuit was about fifteen centimetres across and two centimetres thick, so it kept Robbie quiet for a long time. For both of them an egg was a rare treat, and they'd never had two each before.

By evening, Rob and Elspeth knew their way around the ship. They heard plenty of angry complaints about the crowded holds and makeshift washrooms, but they thought nothing of it because they had shared a toilet with five other families back in Glasgow.

Robbie didn't want to sleep, with all the excitement and noise. On one side of them a baby was crying. On the other, a man and his wife were arguing.

"I'll lie down here right beside you," Elspeth said, tucking a blanket around Robbie. "Look, here's Pig-Bear!"

The quarrelling voices became still, and they could hear the mother singing softly to her crying baby. Tears filled Elspeth's eyes as she recognized the sweet, sad music of "Bonny Doon," a song that Mama used to sing. "Ye mind me of departed joys, departed never to return." Elspeth began to cry.

Robbie reached up and touched Elspeth's wet cheek. "Don't cry, Elspeth!" he said softly. "*They'll* never find us here. *They* won't know where to look."

She snuggled closer to him. Was it easier or harder for Robbie, not being burdened with so many memories? she wondered. As time went by, he would forget Mama and Papa. But at least he still had her, and she had him. Comforted by this thought, she finally drifted off to sleep to the soothing sound of hymns.

For the first time since Mama had died, Robbie slept through the night. They were awakened by the sounds of the families around them beginning their second day at sea. Elspeth went to wash a few clothes in a scant bucket of water one of the stewards had provided, leaving Robbie behind. When she returned to the hold she was surprised to find that he was not alone. Two freckle-faced girls stared up at Elspeth. They both had fine, light-red hair, almost orange, twisted into tight braids. They looked about eight or nine years old. Elspeth was sure she had seen them before.

"They're Rachel and Rebecca," Robbie said eagerly. "They want to be Shadow Bairns."

"Shadow Bairns are quiet," Elspeth said sternly. "How do they know about Shadow Bairns if *you* were quiet?"

"Pig-Bear went out and that one—Rachel—found him. I had to go out and get him. Shadow Bairns stick together."

Elspeth looked at the girls and wondered how Robbie knew which one was Rachel. They looked exactly alike. Then she remembered where she had seen them before. At Carlisle Station, with their father and mother and brother, saying goodbye to the old ladies.

"Please, will you let us be Shadow Bairns?" Rebecca asked.

"Let them," Robbie pleaded.

Elspeth looked at his eager face. It might help to have friends on the boat, even though they were younger than she was. And playing with them would keep Robbie amused. "All right," she said.

"I knew she'd let us! I knew she would!" Rachel said to Robbie.

"But first you have to show that you know *how* to be Shadow Bairns. You have to creep through the hold and up to the deck and hide behind the lifeboat near the top of the stairs without your brother seeing you."

"How do you know about our brother?" Rebecca asked.

"Elspeth knows everything," Robbie answered proudly. "I'll show you the lifeboat."

Elspeth watched them go, looking forward to a few minutes to herself. Robbie and the twins merged with the shadows, passing through the hold with exaggerated caution, but no one paid any attention to them. It was easy to be a Shadow Bairn! Easy to go unnoticed, even in a place where there wasn't enough room for everyone. Elspeth suddenly found that she didn't want to be alone after all. Taking the clothes she had just washed, she followed the children to the deck, giving them time to reach the lifeboat first.

They had pulled a piece of loose canvas around them to shut out the wind, and were sitting together, snug in its shelter.

"We did it! We did it!" shouted one of the twins.

"Shadow Bairns are quiet," Elspeth reminded her.

"Tell us more about Shadow Bairns."

Elspeth sat down beside them and told them about this place called Manitoba where the Shadow Bairns were going. She could see the place clearly just from the sound of its name. It was a small town, with steep mountains behind, close to a huge lake, like the picture Miss Johnstone had shown them. The houses were white, crowded close together, and had steep red roofs and doors of different colors.

"What color is Uncle Donald's door?" Robbie asked.

"Blue," Elspeth answered. "Blue like the water in the lake. And all around the lake are beaches of silver sand."

The story was interrupted by an angry shout. "So that's where you brats are hiding! I should throw you overboard, because that's where Papa and Mama think you are by now, and I'm getting the blame for it! You come back down to your bunk and stay there!"

"We can't, Matthew! We're Shadow Bairns," said Rachel.

"We weren't to tell," shouted Rebecca.

The boy grabbed the twins and pulled them toward the stairs, both of them yelling loudly.

"Maybe their brother wants to be a Shadow Bairn too," Robbie suggested when they were gone.

Elspeth shook her head. He was too old to pretend things like that. Besides, he hadn't even noticed her and Robbie.

"I'm hungry," Robbie said.

"Maybe there are still some eggs and biscuits," Elspeth answered hopefully. "Let's go down to the dining room."

The stewards were bringing in pots of stew and mashed potatoes. Elspeth and Robbie hesitated in the doorway, drawn by the warm smell of the food, but afraid to go into the crowded dining room.

"Have your ma and pa lost their appetites already?" a friendly steward asked. "Come on in and help yourselves."

They filled their bowls and sat close together at one of the big tables, eating quickly and feeling like uninvited guests at a party. The benches were nailed to the floor, and the tables had raised edges that made it difficult for Robbie to reach his food. They soon understood the reason for the raised edges when bowls and mugs slid across the table as the ship rolled.

"Hold on to your dish, Rob," Elspeth warned. Too late. Robbie's plate had shot across the table.

"One bowl of this muck is enough for me!" said the man opposite, pushing it back.

Robbie laughed, and they both began to feel more at ease.

After dinner they went down to the hold. The mother was singing to her baby, and someone was snoring loudly on the other side. Their dark corner now seemed familiar and welcoming. A feeling of well-being settled over Elspeth. She and Robbie were together, part of this huge family of people, all going to Canada.

ABOUT THE AUTHOR
MARGARET JEAN ANDERSON

Margaret Jean Anderson was born in a Scottish coal-mining town, where she began telling stories to her little sister in an effort to coax her to school each day. She later emigrated to Canada, where she held various jobs. After marrying and having children, Jean continued telling stories to entertain her own children. Eventually, she decided to become a writer. At first she wrote non-fiction books, but she has now had several fiction books published, including *The Journey of the Shadow Bairns* and *Searching for Shona*.

Journey to Freedom

by Rosemary Sadlier

Harriet Tubman was born a slave on a plantation near Bucktown, Maryland, about the year 1820. She died over ninety years later in 1913 in Auburn, New York. Harriet led an unbelievable life, actively supporting causes that she felt were just and right, particularly her dedication to guide hundreds of Black freedom seekers out of their slavery to freedom through the Underground Railroad.

With the beginning of the Civil War she took an active part in the cause of the Union side and later in her life she led the causes of temperance and women's rights.

During the 1850s when she was most active in her rescue missions to bring her "passengers" to freedom in the North and to Canada, she lived in St. Catharines, Canada, which was her base.

Harriet Tubman was silently making her way north with a group of twenty-five escaping slaves in the early morning. They were all hungry and tired, and now the heavens had opened up, dropping sheets of rain on the brave group. Only the twin baby girls were oblivious to their circumstances—Harriet had given them a sleeping drug to make sure they stayed quiet.

Suddenly, a feeble light appeared, flickering from the window of what they could barely make out as a cottage. It was the safe house Harriet had promised they would reach. The prospect of some food and shelter from the rain lifted their spirits, and some of the group wanted to run ahead to hug the members of the free Black family that lived there. They were so hungry that even a stale crust of bread would seem like the most wonderful meal in the world!

But Harriet warned them to be quiet, to stay hidden where they were and to remain motionless. Even though she had been welcomed at the safe house before, she knew she had to always be on guard for bounty hunters who were everywhere. She heard the yelp of the hounds and sensed that something was not quite as it should be. Maybe it was the way the lamp was placed in the window—usually it was in the centre of the window, but tonight it wasn't.

Cautiously, Harriet approached the door of the cottage and knocked in her special way to give the secret signal. After a time, a White man opened the door and demanded to know what she wanted. Harriet had to think fast. If she didn't give him some reasonable answer, he would surely be suspicious. She was looking for a friend of hers, she said. The man replied that her friend no longer lived there, that he had been obliged to leave because he had been involved in helping slaves escape. Harriet thanked him for the information and quickly turned away.

Harriet knew that it would be only a matter of moments before the man realized that she might be a runaway slave seeking shelter. When he did realize this, he would certainly alert others who would come looking for her and her charges with horses and wagons, even dogs.

Dawn was fast approaching when Harriet suddenly remembered that there was a small island in the middle of a nearby swamp, with tall grass that would conceal them. The exhausted

TO BE SOLD & LET
BY PUBLIC AUCTION,
On MONDAY the 18th of MAY, 1829,
UNDER THE TREES.
FOR SALE,
THE THREE FOLLOWING
SLAVES,
VIZ.
HANNIBAL, about 30 Years old, an excellent House Servant, of Good Character.
WILLIAM, about 35 Years old, a Labourer.
NANCY, an excellent House Servant and Nurse.
The MEN belonging to "LEECH'S" Estate, and the WOMAN to Mrs. D. SMIT

TO BE LET,
On the usual conditions of the Hirer finding them in Food, Clothing and Medical Assistance.
THE FOLLOWING
MALE and FEMALE
SLAVES,
OF GOOD CHARACTERS.
ROBERT BAGLEY, about 20 Years old, a good House Servant.
WILLIAM BAGLEY, about 18 Years old, a good House Servant.
JOHN ARMS, about 18 Years old.
JACK ANTONIA, about 40 Years old, a Labourer.
PHILIP, an Excellent Fisherman.
HARRY, about 27 Years old, a good House Servant.
LUCY, a Young Woman of good Character, used to House Work and the Nursery;
ELIZA, an Excellent Washerwoman.
CLARA, an Excellent Washerwoman.
FANNY, about 14 Years old, House Servant.
SARAH, about 14 Years old, House Servant.

Also for Sale, at Eleven o'Clock,
Fine Rice, Gram, Paddy, Books, Muslins,
Needles, Pins, Ribbons, &c. &c.
AT ONE O'CLOCK, THAT CELEBRATED ENGLISH HORSE
BLUCHER,

101. 1829 AUCTION SALE
15 × 12" approx. Addison. Place unknown.
This leaflet announcing the sale of slaves presumably
comes from the United States of America, from one
of the southern states, or possibly from the West
Indies.

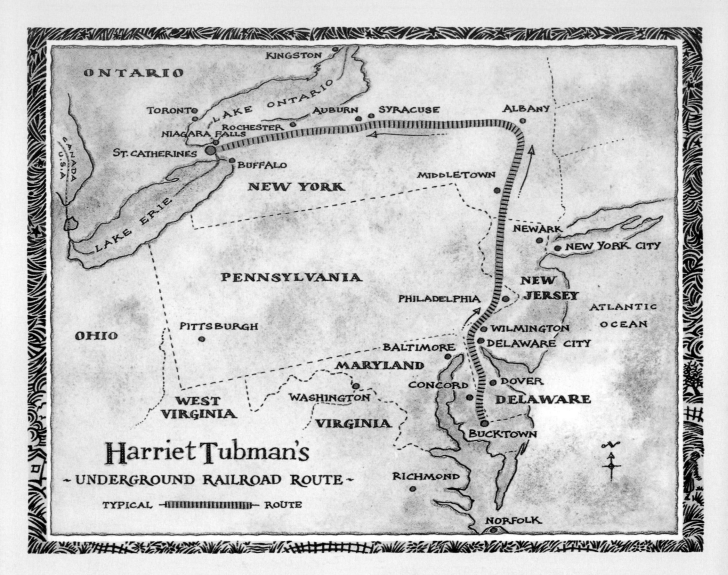

Harriet Tubman's
~UNDERGROUND RAILROAD ROUTE~

TYPICAL ▦▦▦▦▦▦ ROUTE

party waded to the island and Harriet ordered them to lie down in the grass. They obeyed, knowing that their very lives depended on following her instructions. Harriet considered going off by herself to find food, as they hadn't eaten. What to do?

She decided not to risk exposing the group. The deeply religious Harriet began a silent prayer, hoping and expecting that in due course the needs of her charges would be taken care of. All through the morning and afternoon, she prayed. Finally, at dusk, a man dressed like a Quaker walked slowly along the pathway just across from where her frightened group huddled still and quiet. He seemed to be talking to himself, and as he got

closer, Harriet heard him say, "My wagon stands in the barnyard of the next farm across the way. The horse is in the stable, the harness hangs on a nail." He then continued on his way.

When darkness fell, Harriet left the group to investigate the farm the man had mentioned and discovered that indeed the horse and wagon were there, along with a good supply of food, which had been placed in the wagon. She quickly gathered her passengers together in the wagon and made her way to the nearby town. There, another Underground Railroad station master helped her and the group on the next leg of their journey to freedom to the North.

Underground Railroad Terms

The terms used for the Underground Railroad came into use about the year 1840, although slaves had been escaping north before this time. The mid-1800s was a period in which railroads were being constructed in North America as well as elsewhere in the world. Railroad terms seemed appropriate to signal the various aspects of secrecy surrounding the Underground Railroad—and to confuse slave catchers. The following are some of the terms used:

Conductor: A person who would guide freedom seekers from one station to another along a track of the Underground Railroad.

Drinking Gourd: The North Star was referred to as the "Drinking Gourd." The North Star had a constant position in the sky and could be depended upon to provide direction for people at night during their travel.

Freedom Seekers: Enslaved Africans who were determined to be free.

Passengers, Cargo, or Freight: The coded terms that referred to runaway slaves.

Station: A safe house or area where freedom seekers could find food and/or shelter. In many cases the escapee would hide in a root cellar or a hidden room or barn. Although there was no master plan, stations were often located about twenty-five kilometres apart.

Station Master: The person who would watch for freedom seekers, provide them with clothing and food and give them information on the route the freedom seekers should follow on the next stage of their journey.

Stockholders: People who helped freedom seekers by donating money, food, clothing, or any item that could be used.

Terminal: The final destination of the freedom seekers.

Track: A route on the Underground Railroad.

ABOUT THE AUTHOR ROSEMARY SADLIER

Rosemary Sadlier is a sixth-generation Canadian who was born and educated in Toronto. She is the author of numerous articles for magazines, newsletters, and newspapers, and has also written four books on the African-Canadian experience, including *Leading the Way: Black Women in Canada* and *Mary Ann Shadd*. Rosemary is the President of the Ontario Black History Society and is a frequent presenter at schools and libraries on the African-Canadian experience.

Ginger for the Heart

by Paul Yee
Illustrated by Carmen Ngai

The buildings of Chinatown are stoutly constructed of brick, and while some are broad and others thin, they rise no higher than four solid storeys. Many contain stained-glass windows decorated with flower and diamond patterns, and others boast balconies with fancy wrought-iron railings.

Only one building stands above the rest. Its turret-like tower is visible even from the harbor, because the cone-shaped roof is made of copper.

In the early days, Chang the merchant tailor owned this building. He used the main floor for his store and rented out the others. But he kept the tower room for his own use, for the sun filled it with light. This was the room where his wife and daughter worked.

His daughter's name was Yenna, and her beauty was beyond compare. She had ivory skin, sparkling eyes, and her hair hung long and silken, shining like polished ebony. All day long she and her mother sat by the tower window and sewed with silver needles and silken threads. They sang songs while they worked, and their voices rose in wondrous harmonies.

In all Chinatown, the craftsmanship of Yenna and her mother was considered the finest. Search as they might, customers could not discern where holes had once pierced their shirts. Buttonholes never stretched out of shape, and seams were all but invisible.

One day, a young man came into the store laden with garments for mending. His shoulders were broad and strong, yet his eyes were soft and caring. Many times he came, and many times he saw Yenna. For hours he would sit and watch her work. They fell deeply in love, though few words were spoken between them.

Spring came and boats bound for the northern gold fields began to sail again. It was time for the young man to go. He had borrowed money to pay his way over to the New World, and now he had to repay his debts. Onto his back he threw his blankets and tools, food and warm jackets. Then he set off with miners from around the world, clutching gold pans and shovels.

Yenna had little to give him in farewell. All she found in the kitchen was a ginger root as large as her hand. As she stroked its brown knobs and bumpy eyes, she whispered to him, "This will warm you in the cold weather. I will wait for you, but, like this piece of ginger, I, too, will age and grow dry." Then she pressed her lips to the ginger, and turned away.

"I will come back," the young man said. "The fire burning for you in my heart can never be extinguished."

Thereafter, Yenna lit a lamp at every nightfall and set it in the tower window. Rains lashed against the glass, snow piled low along the ledge, and ocean winds rattled the frame. But the flame did not waver, even though the young man never sent letters. Yenna did not weep uselessly, but continued to sew and sing with her mother.

There were few unmarried women in Chinatown, and many men came to seek Yenna's hand in marriage. Rich gold miners and sons of successful merchants bowed before her, but she always looked away. They gave her grand gifts, but still she shook her head, until finally the men grew weary and called her crazy. In China, parents arranged all marriages, and daughters became the property of their husbands. But Chang the merchant tailor treasured his daughter's happiness and let her be.

One winter, an epidemic ravaged the city. When it was over, Chang had lost his wife and his eyesight. Yenna led him up to the tower where he could feel the sun and drifting clouds move across his face. She began to sew again, and while she sewed, she sang for her father. The lamp continued to burn steadily at the tower window as she worked. With twice the amount of work to do, she labored long after dusk. She fed the flame more oil and sent her needle skimming through the heavy fabrics. Nimbly her fingers braided shiny cords and coiled them into butterfly buttons. And when the wick sputtered into light each evening, Yenna's heart soared momentarily into her love's memories. Nights passed into weeks, months turned into years, and four years quickly flew by.

One day a dusty traveller came into the store and flung a bundle of ragged clothes onto the counter. Yenna shook out the first shirt, and out rolled a ginger root. Taking it into her hand, she saw that pieces had been nibbled off, but the core of the root was still firm and fragrant.

She looked up. There stood the man she had promised to wait for. His eyes appeared older and wiser.

"Your gift saved my life several times," he said. "The fire of the ginger is powerful indeed."

"Why is the ginger root still firm and heavy?" she wondered. "Should it not have dried and withered?"

"I kept it close to my heart and my sweat coated it. In lonely

30

moments, my tears soaked it." His calloused hands reached out for her. "Your face has not changed."

"Nor has my heart," she replied. "I have kept a lamp burning all these years."

"So I have heard," he smiled. "Will you come away with me now? It has taken many years to gather enough gold to buy a farm. I have built you a house on my land."

For the first time since his departure, tears cascaded down Yenna's face. She shook her head. "I cannot leave. My father needs me."

"Please come with me," the young man pleaded. "You will be very happy, I promise."

Yenna swept the wetness from her cheeks. "Stay with me and work this store instead," she implored.

The young man stiffened and stated proudly, "A man does not live in his wife's house." And the eyes that she remembered so well gleamed with determination.

"But this is a new land," she cried. "Must we forever follow the old ways?"

She reached out for him, but he brushed her away. With a curse, he hurled the ginger root into the fireplace. As the flames leapt up, Yenna's eyes blurred. The young man clenched and unclenched his fists in anger. They stood like stone.

At last the man turned to leave, but suddenly he knelt at the fireplace. Yenna saw him reach in with the tongs and pull something out of the flames.

"Look!" he whispered in amazement. "The ginger refuses to be burnt! The flames cannot touch it!"

Yenna looked and saw black burn marks charring the root, but when she took it in her hand, she found it still firm and moist. She held it to her nose, and found the fragrant sharpness still there.

The couple embraced and swore to stay together. They were married at a lavish banquet attended by all of Chinatown. There, the father passed his fingers over his son-in-law's face and nodded in satisfaction.

Shortly after, the merchant Chang died, and the young couple moved away. Yenna sold the business and locked up the tower room. But on nights when boats pull in from far away, they say a flicker of light can still be seen in that high window. And Chinese women are reminded that ginger is one of their best friends.

ABOUT THE AUTHOR   PAUL YEE

Born in Saskatchewan, Paul Yee grew up in Vancouver's Chinatown. He received a Master of Arts degree in history from the University of Bristish Columbia. Paul went on to write many magazine articles, short stories, poems, and books, including *Roses Sing on New Snow*. Most often Paul writes about Chinese Canadians for adults and children. His advice to new writers is "to know why you want to write and figure out what you have to say that is unique."

The Doukhobors

Doukhobors are Russian people who escaped Russia in the nineteenth century. The reason they left was because they were going to have to go in the czarist army, but their religion had a law never to fight. Canada welcomed the Doukhobors and they continued their way of life here. The most interesting thing is that often they are very isolated from the world beyond their villages, but still, they're very hospitable. Another fact is that many Doukhobors strictly keep all their traditions and beliefs. Even their lifestyle is still much the same as it was in Russia in the nineteenth century.

Doukhobors continued their way of life here. I think their dynasty will continue as long as Canada exists.

Ivan Poukhovski
Grade 6

Where My Family Comes From

I was born in Canada, but I am partially Swedish and English. My Swedish name is Yakov, and my English name is Jacob. My father's mother was Canadian and his father was British. They met when my grandfather came to Canada as a soldier in World War II. He was an airplane pilot. They then went back to England before moving to Canada in 1951, when my father was three years old. Most of my ancestors are from England. My dad still likes food from England like Goldeneye trout and oysters on crackers.

My mother's father and mother are Canadian, but my mother's mother was born in Sweden. She came to Canada when she was a little girl and didn't speak English until she was twelve years old. My grandfather from Sweden was a tank driver in World War II. At Christmas time we eat traditional Swedish foods such as seven different kinds of cookies, and flat bread called Canuck.

Jacob Day
Grade 6

Alexandria Mah

I feel good about my connections with my ancestors in China. I like the traditions we celebrate, such as the Chinese New Year.

Links to China

I was born in Canada, but I'm Chinese. My name in Chinese is Liyee.

My whole family is Chinese. My father's parents were born and raised in China. So were my mother's parents. However, my own parents were born and raised in Canada.

When my father's parents got married, they only got to see each other by photo. Then they moved to Fort Chipewan and opened a restaurant.

Then, when my father and all of my aunties were born (on my dad's side), my grandparents bought a house in Edmonton. My dad was the only boy in his family. My father and mother met and married in Edmonton.

When I was born, we lived in Fort Chipewan for a few years, but now I live in Edmonton.

Most years at Christmas, my three sisters, my mom and dad, and I go visit my Granny in Fort Chipewan. I like learning about my Chinese background from my parents and Granny.

Alexandria Mah
Age 10

Student Writing

33

Bringing the Prairie Home

by Patricia MacLachlan

Place.
This is one of my favorite words, and I am a writer because of it.
Place.

I remember vividly the place where I was born: the smell of the earth, the look of the skies when storms came through; the softness of my mother's hollyhock blooms that grew by the back fence.

When I was ten years old, I fell in love with place. My parents and I drove through the prairie, great stretches of land between small towns named wonderful names like Spotted Horse, Rattlesnake, Sunrise. We stopped once for drinks that we fished out of cold-water lift-top tanks, and my mother and I walked out onto the prairie. Then my mother said something that changed my life forever. She took a step, looked down at her footprint, and said, "Someone long ago may have walked here, or maybe no one ever has. Either way it's history."

I thought of those who might have come before me and those who might come after, but mostly I was face-to-face with the important, hopeful permanence of place, place that I knew was there long before I walked there, and would be there long after I was gone. I realized, in that moment, that the Earth is history. The Earth is like a character who has secrets; the Earth holds important clues to who we are, who we've been; who we will be. We are connected to the land and to those secrets.

It was after this event that I bought a diary and began writing all sorts of truths about myself, as if I, too, might leave clues about myself behind. I was becoming a writer. All because of place. Now I cannot write a story unless I know the place, the landscape that shapes the story and the people in the story. And to remind myself of the place that changed me, I have carried a small bag of prairie dirt with me for years.

I took that bag of prairie dirt with me once to a class of students, and I found that those children are connected to place, too. Some had moved from place to place many times: One boy's house had burned in a fire recently; another was about to move to a place he had never been.

"Maybe," I said, "I should toss this out onto my New England yard. I'll probably never live on the prairie again."

"*No!*" cried a boy, horrified. "It might blow away!"

And then a girl had a suggestion.

"Maybe you should put that prairie dirt in a glass on your windowsill, so you can see it when you write. It would be like bringing the prairie home."

And that is where that little piece of my prairie is today; my place, my past, my landscape; in a glass on my windowsill. I have brought the prairie home so that I can look at it every day; write about it, write about me, and remind myself that the land is the connection that links us all.

ABOUT THE AUTHOR   PATRICIA MacLACHLAN

Patricia MacLachlan's first book, *The Sick Day*, was published in 1979. Since then she has gone on to write many award-winning books for young readers, including *Sarah, Plain and Tall*. She now lives in western Massachusetts, where she spends her days "as a wife, reader, teacher, bird-watcher and cello player on the good days." She also continues to write. Patricia says, "The characters in my books become, for me, good friends, extended family members, or the brothers and sisters I never had."

The Flute Player

by *Ruskin Bond*
Illustrated by Alice Priestley

Down the main road passed big yellow buses, cars, pony-drawn tongas, motorcycles, and bullock-carts. This steady flow of traffic seemed, somehow, to form a barrier between the city on one side of the trunk road, and the distant sleepy villages on the other. It seemed to cut India in half—the India Kamla knew slightly, and the India she had never seen.

Kamla's grandmother lived on the outskirts of the city of Jaipur, and just across the road from the house there were fields and villages stretching away for hundreds of kilometres. But Kamla had never been across the main road. This separated the busy city from the flat green plains stretching endlessly towards the horizon.

Kamla was used to city life. In England, it was London and Manchester. In India, it was Delhi and Jaipur. Rainy Manchester was, of course, different in many ways from sun-drenched Jaipur, and Indian cities had stronger smells and more vibrant colors than their English counterparts. Nevertheless, they had much in common: busy people always on the move, money constantly changing hands, buses to catch, schools to attend, parties to go to, TV to watch. Kamla had seen very little of the English countryside, even less of India outside the cities.

Her parents lived in Manchester, where her father was a doctor in a large hospital. She went to school in England. But this year, during the summer holidays, she had come to India to stay with her grandmother. Apart from a maidservant and a grizzled old night watchman, Grandmother lived quite alone, in a small house on the outskirts of Jaipur. During the winter months, Jaipur's climate was cool and bracing; but in the summer, a fierce sun poured down upon the city from a cloudless sky.

None of the other city children ventured across the main road into the fields of millet, wheat, and cotton, but Kamla was determined to visit the fields before she returned to England. From the flat roof of the house she could see them stretching away for kilometres, the ripening wheat swaying in the hot wind. Finally, when there were only two days left before she went to Delhi to board a plane for London, she made up her mind and crossed the main road.

She did this in the afternoon, when Grandmother was asleep and the servants were in the bazaar. She slipped out of the back door, and her slippers kicked up the dust as she ran down the path to the main road. A bus roared past, and more dust rose from the road and swirled about her. Kamla ran through the dust, past the jacaranda trees that lined the road, and into the fields.

Suddenly, the world became an enormous place, bigger and more varied than it had seemed from the air, also mysterious and exciting—and just a little frightening.

The sea of wheat stretched away till it merged with the hot

blinding blue of the sky. Far to her left were a few trees and the low white huts of a village. To her right lay hollow pits of red dust and a blackened chimney, where bricks used to be made. In front, some distance away, Kamla could see a camel moving round a well, drawing up water for the fields. She set out in the direction of the camel.

Her grandmother had told her not to wander off on her own in the city; but this wasn't the city, and as far as she knew, camels did not attack people.

It took her a long time to get to the camel. It was about a kilometre away, though it seemed much nearer. And when Kamla reached it, she was surprised to find that there was no one else in sight. The camel was turning the wheel by itself, moving round and round the well, while the water kept gushing up in little trays to run down the channels into the fields. The camel took no notice of Kamla, did not look at her even once, just carried on about its business.

There must be someone here, thought Kamla, walking towards a mango tree that grew a few metres away. Ripe mangoes dangled like globules of gold from its branches. Under the tree, fast asleep, was a boy.

All he wore was a pair of dirty white shorts. His body had been burnt dark by the sun; his hair was tousled, his feet chalky with dust. In the palm of his outstretched hand was a flute. He was a thin boy, with long bony legs, but Kamla felt that he was strong too, for his body was hard and wiry.

Kamla came nearer to the sleeping boy, peering at him with some curiosity, for she had not seen a village boy before. Her shadow fell across his face. The coming of the shadow woke the boy. He opened his eyes and stared at Kamla. When she did not say anything, he sat up, his head a little to one side, his hands clasping his knees, and stared at her.

"Who are you?" he asked a little gruffly. He was not used to waking up and finding strange girls staring at him.

"I'm Kamla. I've come from England, but I'm really from India. I mean I've come home to India, but I'm really from England." This was getting to be rather confusing, so she countered with an abrupt: "Who are *you?*"

"I'm the strongest boy in the village," said the boy, deciding to assert himself without any more ado. "My name is Romi. I can wrestle and swim and climb any tree."

"And do you sleep a lot?" asked Kamla innocently.

Romi scratched his head and grinned.

"I must look after the camel," he said. "It is no use staying awake for the camel. It keeps going round the well until it is tired, and then it stops. When it has rested, it starts going round again. It can carry on like that all day. But it eats a lot."

Mention of the camel's food reminded Romi that he was hungry. He was growing fast these days, and was nearly always hungry. There were some mangoes lying beside him, and he offered one to Kamla. They were silent for a few minutes. You cannot suck mangoes and talk at the same time. After they had finished, they washed their hands in the water from one of the trays.

"There are parrots in the tree," said Kamla, noticing three or four green parrots conducting a noisy meeting in the topmost

branches. They reminded her a bit of a pop group she had seen and heard at home.

"They spoil most of the mangoes," said Romi.

He flung a stone at them, missing, but they took off with squawks of protest, flashes of green and gold wheeling in the sunshine.

"Where do you swim?" asked Kamla. "Down in the well?"

"Of course not. I'm not a frog. There is a canal not far from here. Come, I will show you!"

As they crossed the fields, a pair of blue jays flew out of a bush, rockets of bright blue that dipped and swerved, rising and falling as they chased each other.

Remembering a story that Grandmother had told her, Kamla said, "They are sacred birds, aren't they? Because of their blue throats." She told him the story of the god Shiva having a blue throat because he had swallowed a poison that would have destroyed the world; he had kept the poison in his throat and would not let it go further. "And so his throat is blue, like the blue jay's."

Romi liked this story. His respect for Kamla was greatly increased. But he was not to be outdone, and when a small grey squirrel dashed across the path he told her that squirrels, too, were sacred. Krishna, the god who had been born into a farmer's family like Romi's, had been fond of squirrels and would take them in his arms and stroke them. "That is why squirrels have four dark lines down their backs," said Romi. "Krishna was very dark, as dark as I am, and the stripes are the marks of his fingers."

"Can you catch a squirrel?" asked Kamla.

"No, they are too quick. But I caught a snake once. I caught it by its tail and dropped it in the old well. That well is full of snakes. Whenever we catch one, instead of killing it, we drop it in the well! They can't get out."

Kamla shuddered at the thought of all those snakes swimming and wriggling about at the bottom of the deep well. She wasn't sure that she wanted to return to the well with him. But she forgot about the snakes when they reached the canal.

It was a small canal, about ten metres wide, and only waist-deep in the middle, but it was very muddy at the bottom. She had never seen such a muddy stream in her life.

"Would you like to get in?" asked Romi.

"No," said Kamla. "You get in."

Romi was only too ready to show off his tricks in the water. His toes took a firm hold on the grassy bank, the muscles of his calves tensed, and he dived into the water with a loud splash, landing rather awkwardly on his belly. It was a poor dive, but Kamla was impressed.

Romi swam across to the opposite bank and then back again. When he climbed out of the water, he was covered with mud. It made him look quite fierce. "Come on in," he invited. "It's not deep."

"It's dirty," said Kamla, but felt tempted all the same.

"It's only mud," said Romi. "There's nothing wrong with mud. Camels like mud. Buffaloes love mud."

"I'm not a camel—or a buffalo."

"All right. You don't have to go right in. Just walk along the sides of the channel."

After a moment's hesitation, Kamla slipped her feet out of her slippers, and crept cautiously down the slope till her feet were in the water. She went no further, but even so, some of the muddy water splashed on to her clean white skirt. What would she tell Grandmother? Her feet sank into the soft mud, and she gave a little squeal as the water reached her knees. It was with some difficulty that she got each foot out of the sticky mud.

Romi took her by the hand, and they went stumbling along the side of the channel while little fish swam in and out of their legs, and a heron, one foot raised, waited until they had passed before snapping a fish out of the water. The little fish glistened in the sun before it disappeared down the heron's throat.

Romi gave a sudden exclamation and came to a stop. Kamla held on to him for support.

"What is it?" she asked, a little nervously.

"It's a tortoise," said Romi. "Can you see it?"

He pointed to the bank of the canal, and there, lying quite still, was a small tortoise. Romi scrambled up the bank and, before Kamla could stop him, had picked up the tortoise. As soon as he touched it, the animal's head and legs disappeared into its shell. Romi turned it over, but from behind the breast-plate only the head and a spiky tail were visible.

"Look!" exclaimed Kamla, pointing to the ground where the tortoise had been lying. "What's in that hole?"

They peered into the hole. It was about half a metre deep, and at the bottom were five or six white eggs, a little smaller than a hen's eggs.

"Put it back," said Kamla. "It was sitting on its eggs."

Romi shrugged and dropped the tortoise back on its hole. It peeped out from behind its shell, saw the children were still present, and retreated into its shell again.

"I must go," said Kamla. "It's getting late. Granny will wonder where I have gone."

They walked back to the mango tree, and washed their hands and feet in the cool clear water from the well; but only after Romi

had assured Kamla that there weren't any snakes in the well—he had been talking about an old disused well on the far side of the village. Kamla told Romi she would take him to her house one day, but it would have to be next year, or perhaps the year after, when she came to India again.

"Is it very far, where you are going?" asked Romi.

"Yes, England is across the seas. I have to go back to my parents. And my school is there, too. But I will take the plane from Delhi. Have you ever been to Delhi?"

"I have not been further than Jaipur," said Romi. "What is England like? Are there canals to swim in?"

"You can swim in the sea. Lots of people go swimming in the sea. But it's too cold most of the year. Where I live, there are shops and cinemas and places where you can eat anything you like. And people from all over the world come to live there."

Kamla noticed the flute lying on the grass. "Is it your flute?" she asked.

"Yes," said Romi. "It is an old flute. But the old ones are best. I found it lying in a field last year. Perhaps it was the god Krishna's! He was always playing the flute."

"And who taught you to play it?"

"Nobody. I learned by myself. Shall I play it for you?"

Kamla nodded, and they sat down on the grass, leaning against the trunk of the mango tree, and Romi put the flute to his lips and began to play.

It was a slow, sweet tune, a little sad, a little happy, and the notes were taken up by the breeze and carried across the fields. There was no one to hear the music except the birds and the camel and Kamla. Whether the camel liked it or not, we shall never know; it just kept going round and round the well, drawing up water for the fields. And whether the birds liked it or not, we cannot say, although it is true that they were all suddenly silent when Romi began to play. But Kamla was charmed by the music, and she watched Romi while he played, and the boy smiled at her with his eyes and ran his fingers along the flute. When he stopped playing, everything was still, everything silent, except for the soft wind sighing in the wheat and the gurgle of water coming up from the well.

Kamla stood up to leave.

"When will you come again?" asked Romi.

"I will try to come next year," said Kamla.

"That is a long time. By then you will be quite old. You may not want to come."

"I will come," said Kamla.

"Promise?"

"Promise."

Romi put the flute in her hands and said, "You keep it. I can get another one."

"But I don't know how to play it," said Kamla.

"It will play by itself," said Romi.

She took the flute and put it to her lips and blew on it, producing a squeaky little note that startled a lone parrot out of the mango tree. Romi laughed, and while he was laughing, Kamla turned and ran down the path through the fields. And when she had gone some distance she turned and waved to Romi with the flute. He stood near the well and waved back to her.

Cupping his hands to his mouth, he shouted across the fields: "Don't forget to come next year!"

And Kamla called back, "I won't forget." But her voice was faint, and the breeze blew the words away and Romi did not hear them.

Was England home? wondered Kamla. Or was this Indian city home? Or was her true home in that other India, across the busy trunk road? Perhaps she would find out one day.

Romi watched her until she was just a speck in the distance, and then he turned and shouted at the camel, telling it to move faster. But the camel did not even glance at him, it just carried on as before, as India had carried on for thousands of years, round and round and round the well, while the water gurgled and splashed over the smooth stones.

ABOUT THE
AUTHOR RUSKIN BOND

Ruskin Bond was born and raised in India. He still lives in the foothills of the Himalayas, where his windows open out onto the forest and distant snow peaks. He says, "I sit here and, inspired by the life of the hill people and the presence of birds and trees, write my stories and poems." These stories and poems include *Snake Trouble*, *The Eyes of the Eagle*, and the award-winning *The Room on the Roof*. He wrote *Dust on the Mountain* to express his concern for the destruction of the environment in the Himalayas.

Market!

Written and illustrated by Ted Lewin

From the chill highlands of the Andes to the steamy jungles of central Africa, from the fabled souks of Morocco to the tough New York waterfront, people come to market.

They come barefoot and bent with backbreaking loads, walking for days over lonely mountain passes. They come on jungle trails and roads jammed with traffic. They come by dugout canoe from upriver or by trawler after weeks away at sea. They come any way they can.

They come to sell what they grow, catch, or make, and to buy what other people grow, catch, or make.

So come along—let's go to market!

Ecuador
Saquisili, near Ambato

They come, descendants of the Incas, as colorful as tulips with names like Salasacas and Chimborazo. They bring their onions and bitter potatoes grown on terraced slopes that step into the clouds.

They bring their sweaters and ponchos made from the wool of sheep and llamas. Tailors set up shop right on the spot.

They bring bowls made of used tires, and sharp, cane-cutting knives in the shape of crescent moons. They bring rope made of sisal and reeds for thatching. The spice seller takes on the colors of the spices he sells out of old paint cans.

Nepal

Patan, near Kathmandu

They have come for a thousand years over rugged mountain passes, bearing heavy loads held by tumplines on their foreheads or in baskets on poles slung across their shoulders. They bring loads of thatch, potatoes, long radishes and chili peppers, garlic, scallions, sugar cane, and ginger. They set out their balance scales and are ready for business.

Durbar Square bustles with bicycles and motor bikes, holy men and holy cows, people making quiet offerings at elaborately carved shrines, and vendors selling wood carvings, wool carpets and copper pots.

In the square behind the flute sellers, the temples rise to the sky. The mountains beyond rise like white battlements.

Ireland

Ballinasloe, County Galway

They come under wet lead skies, in barrel-shaped wagons as colorful as lacquered Russian boxes. Tough, horse-trading men and fortune-telling women, the Gypsies come with their wealth on the hoof: quick, lean trotters and heavy piebald beauties with round, feathered feet and mad blue eyes.

They camp on the hill beneath the church and sell their horses on the steep, stone steps leading down to the green. Crowded together, the horses are wild and skittish and dangerous.

To show off their horses, the men fluff their feathers with sawdust or ride them bareback down the concrete strip at the foot of the steps, right into the crowd.

A farrier hammers musically on a glowing red horseshoe:

Da da dingdingding
Dingdang
Dingdang
Brrrrringding ding!

The farmers come too—out onto the green as big as four football fields—with big red hunters and shaggy donkeys, Irish draughts, fine-lined jumpers, and tiny Shetland ponies.

The milling sea of horses churns the green into thick, pungent muck. It seems as though all the horses in the world are here: chestnuts, sorrels, bays, blacks, greys. When the sun breaks through, the whites and piebalds dazzle. From the hill above, they look like a great army about to charge into battle.

47

Uganda

Near Kabalega Falls

On a dirt road through the rain forest beneath the Mountains of the Moon, they come. They lead their cows to slaughter, then sell the meat on palm-leaf counters.

They bring tiny bananas, apples, tomatoes, and fat limes, and stack them in neat pyramids under corrugated tin roofs.

They bring smoked fish—big Nile perch—caught at the great Kabalega Falls, near the source of the White Nile.

At the end of the day, all that's left at this crossroad are empty sheds and blood-stained palm leaves.

Fulton Fish Market, New York City

They come while most of us are sleeping, by truck in the black of night. Hard men in rubber boots, mean hooks slung over their shoulders, yell and argue in the artificial day of fluorescent lights. "How much? Whaddaya, kiddin' me?" The first light of morning strikes the old sheds.

Under the snaking highway on the fishy, cobbled street lies a three-metre shark. Fish boxes are scattered like fallen building blocks.

Inside, giant tuna and mako sharks lie on their sides like beached battleships. Men fillet them as skillfully as surgeons. The halibut are bigger than doormats, the sturgeon look like alien life-forms. Red snapper and green dolphin, shellfish and cuttlefish, crayfish and carp. The trucks come, the fish go, all over the city, all over the country.

Morocco
Rissani, near Erfoud

They come to the market at Rissani where, twelve hundred years ago, the Arab city of Sijilmassa grew fat on riches brought from all over Africa–amber, gold, salt, and slaves.

They come from mud-walled towns that rise from the Tafilalet oasis like shoe boxes.

They come astride tiny donkeys that are almost hidden under the enormous loads they carry in saddle baskets: fruit and vegetables, grain and dates.

Through the great gate at Rissani, down narrow, dusty alleys come the overladen donkeys. *"Allez, allez! Attention, attention!"* Get out of the way or be knocked down. For two dirhams they leave their donkeys at the donkey park. At the end of the day, they are somehow able to find their own amid all the kicking, biting, and screaming.

Shafts of light crisscross the dusty dark in reed-covered souks. There are blocks of fat for making soap; folk medicines—dried chameleons, hedgehogs, porcupines, and owls; pottery; clothing; musk.

Berbers, Bedouin, and Tuareg (the "blue men" of the desert) crowd through the arched portals into walled souks, a different sale going on in each: donkeys, sheep, cattle. The traders haggle. There is never a fixed price here.

In the cattle souk, men crowded into tight bunches under the blazing sun argue over prices while their tiny, short-horned cattle wait patiently.

"No, no! You want a camel for a chicken price!" they shout, no matter what they're selling. "What is your *final* offer? I know you are poor, but you have a rich heart."

Date-laden donkeys muscle their way into the date souk, where the dates are as numerous as the flies. Buyers in hooded djellabas hold fat dates in their cupped palms, separating the fruit from the pit with their thumbs.

Beyond the town, beyond the oasis, at the edge of the vast Sahara, rise the great dunes at Merzouga, glowing in the red afternoon light. Two hundred and forty metres high, they curl in sharp ridges and crests like a giant tidal wave that on a whim might bury the oasis, the town, and the market forever.

Crane, Dragon, Tiger
Economic Growth in Asia

by Jo Ann Lévesque
Illustrated by Sue Todd

Today, Asia's economy is progressing at a fantastic rate, and Asian products are reaching all four corners of the globe. Let's take a look at the economies of the continent's major countries and regions.

The Crane

The crane is a national symbol of Japan, and a good image for its high-flying economy. A major competitor of other industrialized nations, Japan is one of the wealthiest countries in the world.

Since the 1950s, Japan has worked hard at achieving its development goals. Because the country has very few natural resources, such as oil, minerals, and lumber, the Japanese government decided to make the most of its greatest strength—its citizens. It made education for all a major priority, and with a highly educated work force, Japan was able to build a solid industrial base. It has also become a leader in technology, especially in the field of electronics.

Unemployment in Japan is low, and Japanese people have one of the highest per capita incomes in the world. Since the prices of Japanese products are fairly stable, families can afford to buy goods and still save some money. In the past, many workers purchased only Japanese goods. This contributed greatly to Japan's wealth because money stayed in the country. Today, though, imports of manufactured goods are rising, because Japanese consumers now purchase many foreign products.

Japan is an economic giant, Asia's most highly developed economy. It has a powerful influence on the economies of many countries around the world. For other Asian nations, Japan's success story is a source of inspiration, and a model for what they hope to achieve in their own economies.

The Dragon

Like the ancient Chinese symbol of the dragon, the People's Republic of China is large and impressive. In area, it is the third largest country in the world. Its population is large too—one out of every five people in the world is Chinese. This huge population creates a tremendous potential market for consumer goods. Because of this, many foreign countries want to invest there.

China became a communist country in 1949. For many years after that, all economic activity was completely controlled by the government. Near the end of the 1970s, however, the government decided to make some major changes in its economic strategy. Private business initiatives were encouraged, and foreign investment was welcomed.

The result? The people's standard of living rose. Farmers' wages tripled, and the number of rural poor was reduced by one-half. Small businesses sprang up in both rural areas and cities. By 1988, the country's main source of income was the sale of manufactured products. In the 1990s, China's economic progress has continued at an even faster rate. In the near future, China will become another economic giant like Japan.

The Tigers

Second only to Japan in economic growth in Asia today are Hong Kong, Taiwan, South Korea, and Singapore. Known as the "four tigers," they have all been extremely flexible and alert in their economic development. They have been quick to follow the example of Japan, and to seize and make the most of every economic opportunity. The tigers are the newly industrialized countries of Asia.

One of the tigers, Hong Kong, consists of two islands and some mainland territory on the southern coast of China. Hong Kong was once a colony of Great Britain, so its economy developed differently from that of the rest of China. Now part of mainland China again, it remains a special economic zone.

Today, high-quality goods manufactured by the tigers are sold around the world. The cost of living and workers' wages in

▲ *Cotton factory in Beijing, China.*

52

these countries are still lower than in older industrialized countries such as Japan or the United States. This means the tigers can produce and sell their goods more cheaply than their competitors.

To avoid this problem, many foreign companies are setting up branches in these countries. This creates still more employment and wealth, helping the tigers' economies grow even faster. Much of the money they make remains at home as investment, for although the people of Hong Kong, Taiwan, South Korea, and Singapore buy goods, they also save money and invest it. The people of Taiwan and Singapore are the biggest savers in the world.

Not everything is perfect in these countries, though. The prices of goods are increasing rapidly. This raises the cost of living for the average worker. Also, some foreign countries are now restricting the entry of the tigers' inexpensive goods into their markets. To maintain their economic momentum, the tigers are seeking out new trade links with other Asian countries. The greatest strength of these economies is their ability to adapt quickly to new situations.

▲ *South Korean picture-tube manufacturer.*

The Bears

The "four bears" of southeast Asia—Thailand, Malaysia, Indonesia, and the Philippines—all have strong economies based mainly on the export of raw materials such as rice, palm oil, wood, tin, and rubber. Many of these natural resources are traded to the tigers and to Japan.

In the past, most of the people in Thailand, Malaysia, Indonesia, and the Philippines worked the land for a living. But that is starting to change. Foreign investment, especially from Japan and the tigers, is creating new opportunities. Japanese companies in particular are very interested in gaining access to markets in these countries, so some of them have formed associations with local companies, or invested in them. This creates jobs for local people. Manufacturing is also increasing rapidly. The income from trade and manufacturing is being invested in such things as roads, electricity, and telephone networks. Health care, sanitation, and education are also priorities.

Some problems remain. The bears must develop their natural resources in sustainable ways, because these resources are the basis for their economies. Also, the bears have some restless neighbors. Vietnam, Cambodia, Laos, and Myanmar have faced serious internal and external conflicts for many years. These conflicts have hindered their own economic development, and may also affect the economies of the four bears as well. That's because both local and foreign companies are wary of setting up businesses in unsettled or unstable conditions.

The Elephants

The elephants are the economies of South Asia. This region includes India, Bangladesh, Pakistan, Nepal, Bhutan, Afghanistan, the Maldives, and Sri Lanka. Although India has many industries, most of the other countries in this region are less developed than other parts of Asia.

South Asia has had a difficult past. Most of its countries were colonized by foreign nations at one time or another. Wars have been fought over territory, and peoples divided when new national boundaries were established. This past still influences the present, so peace is the most basic requirement for economic growth in this region.

A large number of the people of South Asia are farmers, so the sale of agricultural products is the main source of income. And much income is needed, because the region is already home to 1.5 billion people. By the year 2000, South Asia will have around 2 billion people, all of them needing food, health care, and education.

The region has other problems too. One is that there is not enough land for many of its farmers to make a good living. South Asia is also subject to natural disasters such as floods and droughts, which destroy crops and kill many people. India, for example, must spend around one billion dollars per year to repair the damage caused by the annual monsoon storms.

In spite of all this, economic development is going ahead. Irrigation systems are being improved and storage capacity increased in order to keep harvests safe from natural disasters such as floods and typhoons. New techniques are being developed to increase harvests, and roads, electrical grids, and communications networks are being built.

Today, industries are being developed, and many of the people in this region are getting an education. Local companies now process agricultural products in their factories, and the money from the sale of these products helps develop still more industries. Foreign investment has been encouraged too, but in most cases it is controlled by the government. The goal of all the countries in South Asia is to sell more processed products and fewer agricultural products on the international market.

The Tuna

The tuna are three groups of islands in the Asian South Pacific: Melanesia, Micronesia, and Polynesia. Within these groupings are several small countries and territories. The tuna are situated right in the middle of the ocean, far away from the rest of the world. Transportation costs are very high, and the countries in this region are small, so the development of their industries has been limited so far.

In this economic region, people work mostly in agriculture and fishing. On the international market, these countries sell mainly sugar cane, coffee, coconut, cacao, and fish. In the early 1980s, the prices of these products fell on world markets—and so did per capita incomes in this region. Since 1988, though, the prices of these foodstuffs have begun to rise. Economic reforms are bringing in new investors. The future is looking brighter.

Progress Is Catching!

Today, economic growth is spreading through the entire Asian continent. People are better educated, in better health, and are more productive in their work. As a result, their societies are becoming wealthier and better organized, and people's living conditions are improving.

All of this takes time. Asia is vast and complex. Its sheer size and natural barriers, a rapidly increasing population, the lack of natural resources in many countries, the heavy toll of history, unforeseen political developments—all these factors can influence its economic growth. But as you have seen, Asia is on the move—it is opening up and developing. The twenty-first century will belong to Asia.

▲ A BMW assembly line in Vietnam.

◀ Petrochemical company in Shanghai, China.

Now That's OLYMPIC HISTORY!

by Nancy Bonnell-Kangas
Illustrated by Dusan Petricic

Believe it or not, the Olympics all started with one foot race. Greek citizens met in the ancient village of Olympia to honor the Greek god Zeus—and to find out who was the fastest runner in the land! The first record of an "Olympic champion" was set back in 776 B.C., when a young man named Coroebus won the 200 m dash. Records show that the ancient Olympiads were held for thousands of years, every four years, until the year 261 A.D. At that time, wars broke out and the stadiums and buildings in Olympia were destroyed. Later, Olympia was either buried by an earthquake or submerged underwater when a nearby river changed its course. All signs of the ancient sports vanished from sight—until 1875. That's when archaeologists discovered the ruins of Olympia. At the same time, Baron Pierre de Coubertin, a French aristocrat, was looking for a way to get young French kids in shape. He believed that a modern Olympics could do that and could also encourage international goodwill. So, in 1896 the first modern Olympic Games were held. Where? In Athens, Greece, of course! If the ancient Greeks saw an Olympic event today—thousands of years later with all its athletes, new sports, crowds, TV crews, and hoopla—they'd simply drop their javelins and ogle!

- One wrestling champion, Milo of Kroton, supposedly ate 9 kg of bread and drank 10 L of wine a day to train for his gruelling matches. Legend has it that two ancient Greek athletes once ate two whole oxen in one sitting (one each).

- In one ancient Olympic horse race, a mare named Breeze flew to the finish line—while leaving her rider at the starting gate!—and claimed the first-place prize.

- To make themselves as unpleasant as possible, wrestlers in ancient Greece coated their bodies with olive oil and sand.

- Naim Suleymanoglu was known as "Pocket Hercules" because he was just 152 cm tall and 59.9 kg but he could lift three times his body weight.

- The oldest Olympic competitor was seventy-two-year-old Oscar Swahn from Sweden. He won a silver medal in the "running deer shooting" event in 1920.

- What's with the pentathlon? Athletes must ride a horse, fence, shoot a pistol, swim, then run to victory. Apparently the idea is based on what a soldier-messenger might be forced to do in an emergency: carry the news on horseback, fend off enemies, and swim or run to finally deliver the message.

THE TORCH

During the ancient Olympics a flame burned in honor of Zeus. In 1928, the first modern torch was lit. In 1936, the tradition of the torch was taken a few steps further—it was carried to Berlin from Olympia by a relay of more than three thousand torch-bearing athletes. Since then, the Olympic torch has flown, sailed, and it has even been lit by a flame-lighting laser!

THE RINGS

The Olympics' founder, Pierre de Coubertin, saw five interlocking rings on an emblem while he was in Greece and he thought it would make a perfect symbol for the Olympics. Five rings for the world's five continents, interlocked in friendship. The colors—blue, black, red, yellow, and green—were chosen because at least one of these colors is in every nation's flag.

THE FLAG

The official Olympic flag has five rings floating in a field of white, with a gold fringe around the edge. The first flag was made for the 1920 Antwerp Games and it flew over every Olympics until it wore out in 1988. At the end of every Olympics, the mayor of the host city hands the flag over to the mayor of the next host city.

THE MEDALS

Nowadays, athletes "go for the gold," but they used to go for the silver! Why? Long ago, people thought gold was too tacky and not good enough for the dignified Olympics! Gold medals weren't given until 1908. Back then, the second-place winner got a bronze medal and the third-place winner didn't get anything at all.

THE WREATH

Officially, the ancient Olympic prize was a bunch of twigs. It was a wreath of wild olive leaves that had been specially cut with a gold knife by a child. If that seems like a raw deal, think about this: winners became such heroes that they often got free food for life and lots of poems written about how great they were!

THE PLATFORM

When you won in ancient Games, somebody simply shouted out your name, then yelled out your father's name, and then the name of your country. Today, you get to stand on a platform in front of adoring fans, with a medal around your neck, while your country's flag is raised and the national anthem is played.

CLOSING MARCH

In 1956, seventeen-year-old John Ian Wing wrote a letter to the Olympic heads. He said that since the Games open with teams marching under the flags of their individual nations, the Games should close with everyone marching in one big bunch. That way, "the whole world could be one nation." Athletes have mingled at the end of the Olympics ever since.

OLYMPIC RULES

Attention Olympic hopefuls! For health and safety reasons, some sports today have age requirements. You must be at least fourteen to enter bobsled, gymnastics, and diving events; fifteen to enter judo; sixteen for luge and equestrian sports; and seventeen to lift weights and wrestle. But to play soccer, you must be younger than twenty-three years old!

- Fourteen-year-old Nadia Comaneci received the first perfect score (a "10") ever given in Olympic gymnastics for her performance on the uneven parallel bars. The scoreboard actually showed a "1.00," which temporarily stunned the crowd. The very same day, she was awarded her second perfect score. By the end of the Olympics, she racked up no less than seven 10s.

- Some said Italian Attilio Pavesi always bicycled with a bib stuffed with spaghetti, pastries, bananas, and cheese sandwiches—so he'd never go hungry on a ride!

- In 1924, Paavo Nurmi, the "Flying Finn," ran the 1500 m race, set a world record, and got a gold. Then he went to the locker room to take a brief hour's rest. He got up, ran the 5000 m race, set a world record, and got another gold!

- In 1972, American Mark Spitz won seven gold medals—the most anyone has ever won at a single Olympics—and set seven world swimming records.

- New events at Atlanta's 1996 Olympics: mountain biking, beach volleyball (which was played on an artificial field of sand), and women's softball.

- Dawn Fraser was pretty nervous about swimming in the Olympics. When she got to the pool and took off her warm-up suit, she realized that she'd forgotten to put on her swimsuit! Oops!

- Abebe Bikila, a bodyguard for the Ethiopian Emperor, ran the entire 1960 marathon barefoot. What's more, he won! In 1964, he won again (this time, wearing shoes).

- Forgotten events: the baseball throw (played in 1932), tug of war, mountain climbing, choral singing, fishing, and bowling on the green. Before the ancient Games fell apart, there were even poetry and music contests in the Olympics.

- Vassily Alexeyev, the 152 kg weight lifter, was seen eating a breakfast of steak and twenty-six eggs! Maybe that was his secret—he won gold in both the 1972 and 1976 Olympics.

- The father of a French freestyle swimming champion charged into the water—beret and all!—to congratulate his swift son who'd just won the race.

- In 1896, at a mere ten years old, Dimitrios Loundreas of Greece won Olympic medals in the gymnastic competitions.

- Curling, snowboarding, and women's hockey were added to the 1998 Winter Olympic Games.

- The standard high jump "scissor kick" just didn't work for Dick Fosbury. So, he invented his own way to get over the bar: headfirst. Everyone thought this looked ridiculous so they called the move the "Fosbury Flop." But Dick had the last laugh—he left the 1968 Olympics with the gold! Nowadays, most high jumpers flop just like Mr. Fosbury!

- Lew Sprague deserved a medal. He was the guy in charge of feeding all the Olympic athletes (and staff) in Atlanta in 1996. We're talking sixty thousand meals a day, all day, for thirty-three days in a row. That's over one million meals! And he served this food in a dining room, bigger than two football fields, that seated thirty-five hundred people!

Sports!

Children from many different countries like the same sports. I have five pen pals from around the world, and three of them wrote to me about their favorite sports. Merike from Finland told me she likes these sports: horseback riding, football, volleyball, running, and skating. Another one of my pen pals, Heidi, from Finland, told me she likes horseback riding, skiing, hockey, skating, and football. Leanne from England wrote to me that her favorite sports are basketball, netball, swimming, badminton, soccer, volleyball, rugby, skating, Rollerblading, and dancing. My favorite sports are dancing, horseback riding, hockey, swimming, basketball, and skating. I think horseback riding is so popular bacause horses look so cute and gentle that you just want to be near them. Heidi, Leanne, and I like hockey very much, and I think the reason is that hockey is full of action and surprises. I think the reason all four of us like skating is because there are a lot of great skaters out there, and we want to be like them. So, these are some of the sports that people like all around the world

Michelle West
Grade 6

The Olympics— A Common Link

Athletes come from far and near,
From China, Brazil, and Zaire.
They all are very much alike,
Whether swimming, skiing, or on a bike.
They can be running in heavy soles,
But everyone knows they have very high goals.
They represent their countries and compete
    for first place,
All different cultures but the same human race.

Eden Michaelov
Grade 6

I enjoy writing because I like to put down on paper my experiences and feelings. I also very much enjoy creating my own stories, which I then read to my little brothers and sister.

Justin Johnson

Our School's Trip to Boucherville

We all arrived at our school in Waterloo, Ontario, early one Monday morning. At the beginning of this school trip to Boucherville, Quebec, which is south of Montreal, we made a human chain and passed our luggage to the back of the bus. We set off to Toronto to catch the train to Quebec.

After the long train journey to Montreal we took a bus to our pen pals' school, the Louis-Hippolyte-Lafontaine School, where we met all our pen pals in person. After a huge dinner, we left to spend our first night at our pen pals' houses, which was excellent as it helped us to improve our French-speaking skills.

The rest of our visit was spent in Montreal, and there were many things to see and do. We visited the Botanical Gardens, the Insectarium, the Olympic Stadium, and the Biodome. Another interesting site was the Archaeological Museum, where we saw many different artifacts from the first peoples of Quebec. We also went to the Imax Theatre to watch the movies Alaska and Super Speedway, in French!

All good things must come to an end, so on Thursday we hopped on a bus to the train station, cried "au revoir" to our pen pals, and were on our way home.

Justin Johnson
Grade 6

Keeping the Peace:
The United Nations at Work

by Desmond Morton

A Club for All Countries

What is the United Nations? Well, if you think of the world as a big neighborhood, then the United Nations is the organization that helps everyone live together in that neighborhood.

You probably have lots of families in your neighborhood. Some are big, while others have only one or two people in them. Some are well-off and some have a hard time making ends meet. Most of the families seem to live at peace with themselves and their neighbors. Others always seem to be fighting. But one thing almost all families have in common is pride. They don't want other people telling them how to run their lives. If these families were countries, you could call their right to manage their own affairs their sovereignty.

Of course a family's independence has limits. Everyone has to obey the law. You can't hurt people or steal. There are even laws to stop people from making a lot of noise at night. If anyone breaks the law, someone will call the police. Even within a family, police can step in to stop violence. In your neighborhood there are probably people who help when others get sick or when a family runs out of money. There are schools and parks. As well, people elect governments to provide law, order, and many other things.

The Big Neighborhood

The world is the biggest neighborhood you know. It has almost two hundred countries. Some nations are huge. The nations with the most people are China, with 1.2 billion people, and India, with 883 million. The biggest in area is Russia, which covers 17 075 400 km². Canada is second largest, with 9 958 319 km² but only 27 million people. Some countries are tiny. One of the smallest nations, San Marino, has 23 thousand people and covers only 25 km².

The world is not like your neighborhood. There isn't a world government to keep law and order. Instead, the world is like a big schoolyard, but one where no one has the power to stop fights or keep gangs or bullies from hurting other kids. That's why wars and fighting and stealing have gone on forever. It was only fifty years ago, after the worst war ever, that Canada and other countries helped start the United Nations (UN). The members of the UN agreed to work together to stop wars and help each other, but still remain independent countries. In 1997 the UN had 185 member countries. A few more join every year.

For a world organization, the UN is really very small. In 1992–93, the UN budget was only $2.4 billion American. That's only about what the people of Newfoundland spent on their government that year. It would buy the Canadian navy only two new warships. Even though the UN has so little money, people want it to stop wars, feed the hungry, and fight terrible diseases like AIDS.

No wonder some people call the UN a complete failure. However, in its first fifty years the UN has performed miracles.

The Struggle Against War

What can the UN do for peace? Through decisions and resolutions in the General Assembly, it tells the world that war is the wrong way to settle arguments. It pleads with its members to limit the number of weapons they have, especially nuclear weapons. It sends the Secretary-General to countries in conflict in order to help opponents reach peaceful agreements. It writes laws for using the ocean and outer space. The UN pressured South Africa to end policies that could only lead to all-out war between its Black and White people.

When a war breaks out between members, the Security Council reminds one or both sides that they have broken their commitment to the UN's Charter. Sometimes the UN can get both sides to stop fighting in a few days. Then the UN can send in observers or peacekeeping troops to separate the warring sides and make sure the fighting doesn't begin again. It can also send in food and medicine for the victims. The UN usually cannot intervene in a civil war, a war in which people of the same country fight each other, but it can prevent other countries from helping either side by sending arms and soldiers.

The UN has three weapons in the struggle against war:
- It encourages members to disarm.
- It supports a world court and new laws to settle arguments.
- It borrows soldiers from its members to keep the peace and, if necessary, to fight for it.

Canadian Peacekeepers

Between 1947 and 1994, more than 120 000 Canadians have served as peacekeepers in every **UN** operation. It can be very dangerous work. On June 19, 1994, Corporal Mark Isfeld became the hundredth Canadian peacekeeper to die on duty since 1950. Isfeld died in Croatia when he was clearing explosive landmines to make an area safe for others.

Peacekeeping takes great courage, and in 1988 Canadian soldiers shared the honor with soldiers around the world of winning the Nobel Peace Prize. Peacekeeping soldiers may be called on to do many tasks. Canadian soldiers stand guard on ceasefire lines or provide communications. Pilots fly in dangerous conditions to provide **UN** workers with food and medical supplies. Members of the Royal Canadian Mounted Police and other police forces help supervise **UN**-sponsored elections.

Disarmament

One of the first things the UN did when it was started was try to get its members to disarm or destroy all their weapons. But neither the East nor the West felt safe enough to do so. There were many discussions about disarmament, sometimes just between the United States and the former Soviet Union, and sometimes involving other countries. However, by talking about all the ways the other side might cheat, disarmament talks may have increased fears. Canadian experts helped by working hard to find ways to check on each side's progress without raising suspicions of spying.

And sometimes there was progress. The UN organized an agreement to ban poison gas and weapons that carry the germs of horrible diseases. Most countries agreed never to test nuclear bombs in the open air (they still tested them in caves or underground).

The arms race did finally end in the 1990s, but UN members couldn't take much credit for stopping it. What really ended it was that the cost of arms made countries go broke. In 1989, the Soviet bloc collapsed. Most of the republics in the old Soviet Union announced their independence. The Cold War was over.

You'd think countries would have learned their lesson. But Soviet countries now desperate for money sold their weapons and technology to other countries at bargain rates. The dream of world disarmament remained a dream and the world needed the UN more than ever.

World Law

Another way the UN tries to keep peace is by making international laws, fair laws that apply to all countries. The idea of world law dates back almost to the time of Christopher Columbus. Since then, countries have accepted many rules of international law. In 1948 the UN's new International Law Commission (ILC) made laws concerning the Holocaust, the mass murder of six million Jews during World War II. The ILC made it a crime called genocide to attempt to destroy a race or entire group of people. At Vienna in 1961, an ILC conference agreed on how ambassadors and their staffs would be treated by host countries. The ILC also wrote rules to protect people who have no country. Other new laws deal with outer space and with the mineral wealth under the oceans.

Like most decisions the UN and its committees have to make, international laws are difficult to agree on. For example, should only countries with shores along the ocean own the rich minerals under the sea? What about poor countries with no ocean coast? As well, countries with a space program have very different ideas about who should control outer space than do countries that can never even afford a seat on a space shuttle.

As for taking disputes to the International Court of Justice, most countries still refuse.

Soldiers and Peacekeeping

All over the world, soldiers in the UN's blue helmets or caps have risked their lives trying to stop wars. In 1988 they received one of the world's highest honors, the Nobel Peace Prize. Canadians were especially proud, because their soldiers and aircrew

The Nansen Medal

The United Nations High Commission for Refugees (UNHCR) gives the Nansen Medal to people or organizations especially helpful to refugees. Canada is the only country ever to win this award. The medal is named in honor of Norwegian explorer Fridtjof Nansen. He gave his time and money to help people forced to flee their

Fridtjof Nansen

countries because of war and political fights. Usually these refugees did not have passports or identity cards, but Nansen persuaded countries to recognize the "Nansen Passport," a special card for refugees.

On November 13, 1986, Governor General Jeanne Sauvé accepted the Nansen Medal on behalf of all Canadians. The medal acknowledges Canada's hospitality to homeless refugees. Canada is also known around the world for recognizing the particular plight of refugee women as they try to care for themselves and their children.

had shared in almost every UN peacekeeping operation since 1948.

What do peacekeepers do? Why do they have to be soldiers? Often, after two sides stop fighting and agree to a truce, each side fears that the other is cheating. Peacekeeping soldiers can see what is happening with a soldier's eye and report the truth. Canadians have been involved with UN peacekeeping in Israel, Lebanon, Yemen, Nicaragua, and Cambodia. (You can read about some of these and others on pages 67–68.)

Another thing UN peacekeepers do is guard the line between warring sides. That's what Canada's Lieutenant General E. L. M. Burns organized between Egypt and Israel in 1956. In Cyprus in 1964, Canadian soldiers helped guard a "Green Line" between Turks and Greeks. Back in 1990, UN soldiers in Nicaragua made it safe for soldiers of one side to give up their weapons without fear of being massacred. UN peacekeepers in Namibia in 1991 and in Cambodia in 1992–93 guarded voting places from attack by the side that expected to lose. Since 1992 in the former Yugoslavia, UN soldiers have tried to keep people from killing one another because of ancient hatreds. In Bosnia they guarded supplies sent by the world to help people survive the war and the bitter weather.

Trying to Make Peace

In Korea in 1950, Iraq in 1990, and Somalia in 1993, the UN tried to make peace rather than simply keep it. When negotiations, threats, boycotts, and blockades don't work, the UN can fight.

But peacekeeping and peacemaking are difficult and expensive. Nothing else the UN does keeps it more in debt.

Sometimes the UN itself makes a hard job worse. Sometimes, because its members cannot make up their minds, the Security Council gives vague orders. Or its members refuse to send enough soldiers to carry out the orders.

Of twenty-seven peacekeeping operations since 1945, very few have led to lasting peace. UN members and people around the world may ask themselves if trying to stop the killing is worth it. But doing nothing is worse.

Roméo Dallaire

A quiet soldier from Quebec, Major General Roméo Dallaire didn't expect to make history when the UN asked him to command its peacekeepers in Rwanda in 1983. But suddenly he found that there was no peace to keep. Rwandans began killing one another, as well as torturing and killing UN soldiers. The UN ordered most of its soldiers to leave Rwanda, but Dallaire, some of his staff, and soldiers from Ghana stayed, despite the fighting and killing all around them. They saved anyone they could and waited until peace returned. Whatever the risks, Dallaire kept trying to get food and medicine to suffering people. It was a desperately dangerous job, but like other Canadian peacekeepers, he accepted the challenge.

Places Where the UN Has Worked for Peace

Palestine

After 6 million Jews died in World War II, many UN members wanted to give Jews their own country, Israel, in Palestine. The Arabs who already lived there saw no reason why a horrible crime in Europe should cost them their homes. However, it was agreed at the UN that Palestine be directed to give Jews a home. War then broke out between Israel and its Arab neighbors as the Palestinians looked for places to live. After much work, the UN was able to arrange a truce and send in military officers, including Canadians, to help both sides stop fighting. The UN also built camps for Palestinians driven from their homes. Israel and its Arab neighbors have fought four wars since 1949, and many Canadians have served in peacekeeping forces on Israel's borders.

Cyprus

When Britain gave up its island colony of Cyprus in the western Mediterranean, fighting soon broke out between the Greeks and Turks who lived there. Greece and Turkey seemed likely to join the fighting, so the UN agreed to send a peacekeeping force, including several hundred Canadians. War broke out again in 1973 when Greeks tried to take over the island and a Turkish army invaded, but again the UN helped establish peace. In 1993, Canada announced that it would withdraw its forces to encourage the two sides to make peace.

The Suez

Israel had even more problems than its wars between the Palestinians and Arabs. For years it had been attacked by fighters from Egypt and it finally struck back in 1956. At the same time, France and Britain were angry that Egyptians had taken over the Suez Canal and they attacked too. Canada's chief UN delegate, Lester Pearson, was given the job of making peace—fast. With the help of Canada's Lieutenant General E. L. M. Burns, he brought in a force of UN soldiers from countries not involved in the war. Canadian soldiers provided communications, a hospital, and many other services the UN's first army needed.

Bosnia/Croatia

When Yugoslavia broke up in 1991, Serbs and Croats who lived in the north began fighting for control of the land. The UN sent in a large army to stop the fighting. Then Serbs, Croats, and Moslems from neighboring Bosnia began fighting for territory far to the south at Sarajevo in Bosnia-Herzogovina. Again the UN tried to stop the killing and to protect food and fuel sent to the hungry, freezing people. Two Canadian regiments were part of the UN force and Major General Lewis Mackenzie, a Canadian soldier, was one of the leaders of the group trying to stop the fighting at Sarajevo.

Iraq/Kuwait

In August 1990, Iraq's leader, Saddam Hussein, sent his army to conquer neighboring Kuwait. When UN threats and boycotts failed to make him withdraw his army, the United States organized a UN force, including Canadians, to protect Iraq's other neighbors and, in January 1991, to free Kuwait. The allied countries won back Kuwait, but Saddam Hussein was still in power and his armies wrecked the little country.

Korea

On June 25, 1950, Communist-controlled North Korea attacked South Korea. The United States demanded that the UN stop the attack. The Soviet delegates, who were also Communists, had already walked out of the UN because the Americans and their allies would not let communist China join the UN. That meant the Soviets weren't on hand to say no to the American demands. So the UN told the United States to stop North Korea. During the war China sent volunteers to help North Korea and there was bitter fighting. Canada sent soldiers, warships, and transport planes, as did fifteen other UN members. Many soldiers were killed before the Korean War ended on July 27, 1953. The UN saved South Korea.

Cambodia

Cambodia is a country that has been torn apart by internal wars for many years. To help bring peace, in 1992–93 the UN organized an election to help Cambodians choose their next government. Canadians were part of the UN force, mostly from Asian countries, that was on hand to prevent the election from being destroyed by one of the warring groups.

I Dream of Peace

Images of War by Children of Former Yugoslavia

Ptica mira
Bird of peace
Marica, 11,
from Sunja

I am speaking to you, the one they forced from the playground and from the street, from the house where you lived and from your childhood room.

As you suffer, I suffer, and my nights are sleepless too. I do not kick the football like before, I do not sing the way I did. I have locked up my bicycle, and I have locked up my smile. I have locked up my games and my childish jokes as well.

Will the waiting be long? I do not want to grow old while still just a child, and I fear for you that, in the wait, the place of your birth will soon be forgotten. Therefore, my friend, welcome to my place. We will share the sea, and the beauty of a summer evening. We will enjoy the singing of the birds and do our homework together.

– Nemanja, 11, from Sutomore

I am not a refugee, but I understand the fear and the suffering of the children.

My father is a Croat, my mother is a Serb, but I don't know who I am.

My brothers, my sisters, my grandparents, my aunts, and my uncles, all are in Croatia. I have not seen them since the start of this horrible war.

More than a year has passed since I heard their voices. And the only link between us are the letters, letters, only letters. . . .

– Lepa, 11, from Belgrade

If only you knew how it feels to have your father in the war. You flee the misery, but misery follows. You hear not a word about your father, and one day everything goes black and there is Daddy at the door. He stays with you a few days and then happiness is gone again.

My heart, it is pounding like a little clock. I can hardly write this because my beloved Daddy is once again not here with me.

– Žana, 12, refugee from Brčko

Uspomene
Memories
Tihomir, 12,
refugee from
Buna, near Mostar

Stop the war and the fighting
for a smile on a child's face.
Stop the planes and the shells
for a smile on a child's face.

Stop all the army vehicles
for a smile on a child's face.
Stop everything that kills and destroys
for a smile of happiness on a child's face.

– Ivana, 11, from Čepin

Rat
War
Amela, 12,
displaced from
Slavonski Brod

It's all so strange! Suddenly, it's so important, everybody asking who you are, what you do, where you come from.

So many people have been killed fighting for justice. But what justice? Do they know what they are fighting for, who they are fighting?

The weather is growing very cold now. No longer can you hear the singing of the birds, only the sound of the children crying for a lost mother or father, a brother or a sister.

We are children without a country and without hope.

– Dunja, 14, from Belgrade

My sister and I were refugees who fled from Moščenica. We stayed in Zagorje with our grandmother. She was always anxious and constantly yelling at us. Day after day, night after night, we waited for our mother to join us. But she never arrived.

One day, I was sitting on the steps of my house when a blue car came down the street. Inside, I saw my mother. I flew toward her, and then I hugged her to me.

When she said that we would be going back home to Moščenica I was filled with happiness. However, when we arrived there, many of the houses were destroyed, and the sight left me heartsick.

I couldn't believe there could ever be life in our town again. Anyone who saw the destruction would feel the same. That is why this dirty war must stop.

– Jelena, 11, from Moščenica

*Hodanje
po ruševinama*
Walking in ruins
Robert, 13,
refugee from
Kotor Varoš

War is the saddest word that flows from my quivering lips. It is a wicked bird that never comes to rest. It is a deadly bird that destroys our homes, and deprives us of our childhood. War is the evilest of birds, turning the streets red with blood, and the world into an inferno.

– Maida, 12, from Skopje

72

When I walk through town, I see strange faces, full of bitterness and pain. Where has our laughter gone? Where is our happiness? Somewhere far, far away from us. Why did they do this to us? We're their kids. All we want is to play our games and see our friends. And not to have this horrible war.

There are so many people who did not ask for this war, or for the black earth that is now over them. Among them are my friends.

I send you this message: Don't ever hurt the children. They're not guilty of anything.

– Sandra, 10, from Vukovar

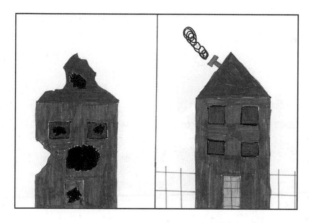

Rat i mir
War and peace
Nataša, 11,
from Pula

War is here, but we await peace. We are in a corner of the world where nobody seems to hear us. But we are not afraid, and we will not give up.

Our fathers earn little, just barely enough to buy five kilos of flour a month. And we have no water, no electricity, no heat. We bear it all, but we cannot bear the hate and the evil.

Our teacher has told us about Anne Frank, and we have read her diary. After fifty years, history is repeating itself right here with this war, with the hate and the killing, and with having to hide to save your life.

We are only twelve years old. We can't influence politics and the war, but we want to live! And we want to stop this madness. Like Anne Frank fifty years ago, we wait for peace. She didn't live to see it. Will we?

– Students from a fifth-grade class in Zenica

To all children throughout the world

I want you to know our suffering, the children of Sarajevo. I am still young, but I feel that I have experienced things that many grown-ups will never know. I don't mean to upset you, but I want you to know that I was staying in Serbian-held territory when my mother and I were put on the list and marked for liquidation. Those of you who live normal lives can't understand such things, nor could I, until I experienced them.

Poruke
Messages
Maja, 12, from Požega

While you are eating your fruit and your sweet chocolate and candy, over here we are plucking grass to survive. When you next have some tasty food, please say to yourself, "This is for the children of Sarajevo."

While you are at the cinema or listening to beautiful music, we are scurrying into basements, and listening to the terrible whine of cannon shells. While you are laughing and having fun, we are crying and hoping that this terror will quickly pass. While you are enjoying the benefits of electricity and running water, and having your baths, we are praying to God for rain so we can have some water to drink.

No film can adequately depict the suffering, the fear, and the terror that my people are experiencing. Sarajevo is awash in blood, and graves are appearing everywhere. I beg you in the name of the Bosnian children never to allow this to happen to you or to people anywhere else.

– Edina, 12, from Sarajevo

The Elders Are Watching

by Dave Bouchard

Illustrated by Roy Henry Vickers

They told me to tell you they believed you
When you said you would take a stand.
They thought that you knew the ways of nature.
They thought you respected the land.

They want you to know that they trusted you
With the earth, the water, the air,
With the eagle, the hawk, and the raven,
The salmon, the whale, and the bear.

You promised you'd care for the cedar and fir,
The mountains, the sea, and the sky.
To the Elders these things are the essence of life.
Without them a people will die.

They told me to tell you the time has come.
They want you to know how they feel.
So listen carefully, look toward the sun.
The Elders are watching.

They wonder about risking the salted waters,
The ebb and flow of running tide.
You seem to be making mistakes almost daily.
They're angry, they're hurting, they cry.

The only foe the huge forest fears
Is man, not fire, nor pest.
There are but a few who've come to know
To appreciate nature's best.

They watch as you dig the ore from the ground.
You've gone much too deep in the earth.
The pits and scars are not part of the dream
For their home, for the place of their birth.

They told me to tell you the time has come.
They want you to know how they feel.
So listen carefully, look toward the sun.
The Elders are watching.

They say you hunt for the thrill of the kill.
First the buffalo, now the bear.
And that you know just how few there are left,
And yet you don't seem to care.

They have no problem with fishing for sport.
There are lots of fish in the sea.
It is for the few who will waste a catch,
For you, they are speaking through me.

You said you needed the tree for its pulp,
You'd take but a few, you're aware
Of the home of the deer, the wolf, the fox,
Yet so much of their land now stands bare.

They told me to tell you the time has come.
They want you to know how they feel.
So listen carefully, look toward the sun.
The Elders are watching.

They're starting to question the things that you said
About bringing so much to their land.
You promised you'd care for their daughters and sons,
That you'd walk with them hand in hand.

But with every new moon you seem to be
More concerned with your wealth than the few
Women and children, their bloodline, their heartbeat,
Who are now so dependent on you.

You are offering to give back bits and pieces
Of the land they know to be theirs.
Don't think they're not grateful, it's just hard to say so
When wondering just how much you care.

They told me to tell you the time has come.
They want you to know how they feel.
So listen carefully, look toward the sun.
The Elders are watching.

Now friend be clear and understand
Not everything's dark and glum.
They are seeing some things that are making them smile,
And that's part of the reason I've come.

The color green has come back to the land.
It's for people who feel like me.
For people who treasure what nature gives,
For those who help others to see.

And there are those whose actions show.
They see the way things could be.
They do what they can, give all that they have
Just to save one ancient tree.

They told me to tell you the time has come.
They want you to know how they feel.
So listen carefully, look toward the sun.
The Elders are watching.

Of all of the things that you've done so well,
The things they are growing to love,
It's the sight of your home, the town that you've built.
They can see it from far up above.

Like the sun when it shines, like the full moon at night,
Like a hundred totems tall,
It has brightened their sky and that's partially why
They've sent me to you with their call.

Now I've said all the things that I told them I would.
I hope I am doing my share.
If the beauty around us is to live through this day
We'd better start watching—and care.

They told me to tell you the time is now.
They want you to know how they feel.
So listen carefully, look toward the sun.
The Elders are watching.

ABOUT THE AUTHOR   DAVE BOUCHARD

Dave Bouchard was born and raised in Saskatchewan. He taught in Regina for several years and now lives and works in Vancouver. His other books include *White Tails Don't Live in the City*, *If You're Not from the Prairie*, and *Voices from the Wild*.

Life in the Military

My opinion on military life is . . . well, it's OK. You get to meet a bunch of new people. You get to attend some nice schools. I find some PMQ's (Permanent Married Quarters) are much better than other ones. The PMQ I live in is one of the better ones, probably because it is a newer model.

The bad things about the military are . . . well, you have to leave all of your friends when your Mom or Dad is transferred. You have to leave your school. You end up having to live in a totally different place, which could be good or bad. I hate all of the moving we have to do, and also the fact that the military could move you anywhere: places you want to go and places you don't. It doesn't matter to them. Overall, I find the military life painful and disturbing!

War and peacekeeping play a large role in a person's military life. My opinion on war and peacekeeping is that it is very painful having your Mom or Dad gone for such a long time. I feel somewhat happy and somewhat not. I feel happy because parents and other people are helping with peace. I feel bad because it seems they leave for a long time. So that is my opinion on war and life in the military!

Zac Organ
Grade 6

I enjoy writing very much because I am able to vent my feelings. I have gone to the young writers' conference twice. Most of my teachers say I am a very creative young person!

Zac Organ

Student Writing

If I Could Wish for One Thing

If I could wish for one thing,
I would wish for peace on Earth for mankind.

If I could wish for one more thing,
I would wish for warm homes for everyone on the street.

If I could wish for another thing,
I would wish for enough food for everyone.

If I could wish for one more thing,
I would wish for a teddy bear for every sad child.

If I had all these wishes,
What a peaceful world it would be.

Malorie Urbanovitch
Age 10

79

The War

Hi. My name is Maryam John. I was born in Afghanistan. When I was only nine years old, there was a war where I lived. The war was with Russia!

One night when we were sleeping we heard an explosion, so we went to see what it was. It was a bomb that had hit the side of our house. When we went back to bed, I couldn't sleep. I was too scared. I could hear my parents talking. They said, for our safety, we had to move from Afghanistan as soon as possible.

After breakfast my father made some phone calls and when he was done he told me and my mom that we were leaving the next day. My mom told me to pack everything up. The day went by quickly. When I went to sleep I was so tired that I overslept. My mom woke me up and told me we had to get dressed quickly because we were going to be late. When we got to the airport I asked my father where we were going. He said, "Canada!" It was a long ride to Canada. I was really bored. When we finally got there I looked around and I knew we had come to a good place. After a couple of weeks my father got a job and my mom went to school and became a teacher. I made lots of friends. My whole family was happy and one of the reasons was that there was no war!!

Meena Hakimyar
Grade 6

I like writing about different things, like medieval times and things that will happen in the future. I usually put my mind to one story until I finish it.

Meena Hakimyar

The Environment

The environment is very important. You need to care for the environment so that the Earth is healthy.

Some ways to care for the environment are to use the three R's (Reduce, Reuse, Recycle), bike or run instead of driving or use environmentally friendly fuel, do not litter, use rubbish bins, compost, plant trees, and so on.

In some places, you can smell an awful smell. That smell is pollution from manufacturing plants. Would you like to live on a foul-smelling planet?

Let's all do our part to help save the world.

Jeff D'Andrea
Grade 6